rediscovering hope and faith after loss

If He
Doesn't

JAZZMINE MAGLOIRE
Foreword by Dr. Denise Rollins

FOREWORD

"Loves God and family, exudes authenticity and is passionate about helping people heal." Those are the words I would have used to describe Jazzmine Magloire many years ago when we first met. As someone who was also following a nontraditional path in a quest to make the world a better place, I was drawn to this intriguing woman who homeschooled her children, was unafraid to be vulnerable as she addressed both her strengths and weaknesses and had a fire in her belly when it came to both her religion and faith. We were very different yet similar, and as I coached Jazzmine in becoming a Whole Heart life coach and facilitator, I sensed she was special.

Yet, as with many relationships, our paths eventually diverged. From time to time, my exposure to Jazzmine consisted of seeing her posts on social media. Those posts painted a consistent picture of Jazzmine: she loves God and family, exudes authenticity, and is passionate about helping people heal. She appeared to live a charmed life, which I sometimes envied because of my own story. When I was 29 years old, a drunk driver killed my mother. Ten years later, my five-month-old son died in a freak accident. Two years later, someone killed my mom's sister drag racing on a public road. And then, two years later, my husband, who was also the father of our four sons, died suddenly. The official diagnosis was sickle-cell disease. Unofficially, I know that grief over our son's death contributed to his early demise. But Jazzmine, unlike me, had a good life and solid faith, as evidenced by her positive posts.

Perhaps that's why it caught my eye when, on social media, I saw Jazzmine's post noting that her son, David, had suffered from a horrible accident. She said she believed in God for his miraculous healing. I stopped and prayed, yet I did not doubt Jazzmine's prayers would be answered because she was powerful. My heart broke days later when she reached out to our funeral home to handle David's services. Even typing those words made my heart ache. Never, ever would I have wanted Jazzmine to join me in the "Land of Broken Mothers." And just like that, I became her coach again. But this time was much more challenging because witnessing her raw pain was both triggering and tragic. Yet it was also transformative to watch her find her footing, stumble at times, cry at others, and question everything she had believed to be accurate. She discovered the newest version of herself and slowly climbed out of the shadow of Death Valley.

I often say that grief magnifies what already exists. That was true of Jazzmine. Her love of God and her family magnified the painful questions about why neither God nor Jazzmine could "save" David. Her authenticity contributed to her asking questions that needed to be discussed but made many people uncomfortable. Her passion for helping people became somewhat of a burden as she questioned whether that focus kept her from noticing things happening in her life.

Moreover, as Jazzmine addressed her grief from death, she simultaneously dealt with her grief from intangible parts of her life (also considered losses) that were painful yet undetectable in her social media posts. From her childhood to young adulthood and marriage, she faced her insecurities, fears, secrets, changes, and more because she realized how necessary it was to escape this valley. As a coach, Jazzmine's magnified grief level became a lens that made me reexamine my pain.

I also believe that the only way to overcome grief is to go through it. And that's what Jazzmine did. She faced the pain and continued to heal, something remarkable to watch. A year ago, I asked Jazzmine about her spiritual journey after struggling with loss. She said she felt that her life's path had come to a dead end after David's passing, and nothing was beyond it. She remembered how she was at the lowest point she'd ever experienced spiritually. Her faith, which used to connect her to others, became something that separated her from other people.

Yet I watched Jazzmine reimagine her whole life, belief system, and path. What emerged was a stronger, wiser, and more resilient person shaped by her love of God and family, her authenticity, and her passion for helping people heal.

That brings us to this precious book in your hands. What I love about Jazzmine telling her story is that she takes us along her journey through hell and back. Feeling her pain, hearing her questions, and understanding her revelations, we, readers, revisit our struggles. We gain knowledge and skills that strengthen us all. Jazzmine does this powerfully in this book, leading us along a path where, like her (and this comes directly from her advice), we can take our pain to God, get quiet as we listen to what He wants to say to us, and what God wants us to know, then live out the promises of Hebrews 4:15-16 NKJV: "For we do not have a High Priest who cannot sympathize with our weaknesses but was in all points tempted as we are, yet without sin. Let us therefore come boldly to the throne of grace, that we may obtain mercy and find grace to help in our time of need." In "If He Doesn't," Jazzmine demonstrates that she, too, sympathizes with our pain and weakness as she shares mercy and grace that will help us in our time of need. May you be as blessed and transformed by Jazzmine's story as I have been!

Denise Rollins, PhD, Author of Wholehearted Grief: A Journey to Find Comfort, Peace & Restoration in the Shadow of Death

Dedicated to Matthew, Jacob, David, Izzy, and JP. You fill my heart with joy and remind me that despite the challenges, I still have much to be thankful for. Love you forever.

Table of Contents

Preface

You can ask God questions, but you can't question God.

- Tony Evans

When you're going through a difficult time in life, you might feel uncertain of yourself and God—wondering where you went wrong or what you've missed. Why isn't God responding? Questions about what you believe begin to surface in these dark nights of the soul. Behind the questions is a broken heart, a wounded soul searching for answers to bring the healing they need. Asking questions might be frowned upon as doubt, but they keep the conversation afloat between you and God.

Negative experiences can be pivotal moments that change the game of what we believe. It's why we change churches, deepen our relationship with God, and struggle with or completely abandon our trust in Him. Our misfortunes can potentially become the soil from which our roots grow deeper. Our challenging questions might prune the dead beliefs we feed on that aren't producing fruit. My goal isn't to tell you what to believe or what to prune but to encourage you to walk through the process. Since coming to Christ when I was 15, I've always asked questions, trying to understand the faith to which I have dedicated my life. I have learned that questions send you on a quest. It wasn't until I lost my son that I couldn't settle for "just believe." Much like successes, disappointments cause you to analyze and modify. Triumph and defeat give shape to our thinking and decision-making. When something doesn't work, you note what to avoid in the future. We do this on the job, at home, and in relationships. We are constantly assessing better ways to live our lives, shaving off the things we tried and failed at, and developing our sweet spots.

As we go through difficulties in life, we evaluate what worked and what didn't, even in terms of our faith. When you pray for the job and get it, a family member turns their life around, or they don't have to perform surgery, you are encouraged to pray more because you saw success! Prayer was answered. In the church world, we call it a praise report. These amazing things inspire us not only to continue doing what we're doing but also to hone it. Conversely, you were fired, there were complications with the surgery, and insurance didn't cover it, or you lost a loved one despite your prayer chain; these life events can have a devastating effect on what you believe.

I hope you can ask questions and hold on to God simultaneously. We can take these significant disappointments and present them to God with questions. While the "why" question may never be answered this side of heaven, there may be other answers God wants to give you. These answers may help you heal and hold on till He returns in His fullness. Sometimes, it's not the answers He intends to provide, but Himself.

If you're trudging through the valley of defeat, I hope you'll find companionship with me through the chapters of this book. In this life, we are met with unexplainable, irrevocable, devastating experiences that make us question the words of Jesus and the words of many sermons. On the following pages, you will not read about how I prayed, and everything turned out exactly how I prayed for it. You will not find a formula for getting what you want in life. No, you will read about my process through the storms of life. It's not a model to repeat, but it encourages you to work through your process. My thoughts aren't churchy, pretty, or neat. I'm not representing, promoting, or denying any denomination. This is about handling life's blows with God for growth and depth instead of destruction and defeat. The changes we pass through and the events that catalyze them. By allowing myself to converse with God through my trauma, I discovered my faith didn't change. However, those questions sat over the top of it. May your questions send you on a quest that leads you to eternal hope, not because everything worked out but because you discovered new meaning when it didn't?

Chapter 1

What if God doesn't?

"One life loss can infect the whole of a life."

Ann Voskamp

Unable to sleep, I paced the hotel floors, nursing our infant. As we waited to hear the following report on whether our 12-year-old, in the hospital next door, would live or if my hug with him earlier that day would be my last, I prayed fervently. All my Christian training on faith was being summoned from the corners of my mind. Trying to remember the "rules' I learned in sermons, conferences, and books, I did not want to do or say anything that could compromise my chances of receiving a miracle. I'm a daughter of God. He has given me power and authority to tread on serpents and scorpions. His power is within me to use at will. Feeling desperate for David to live, I wanted to beg. However, I was instructed that because of who Christ is in me, I don't need to pray or ask God; I need to declare it. The urge to break down and beg God for my son's life welled up inside. Instead, I followed the instructions given to me from previous teaching. I spoke into the atmosphere. I talked to devils I couldn't see but assumed they were around somewhere doing their absolute best to keep my son from coming, too. I told the spirit of death to leave him and commanded David to return like Jesus did Lazarus. I listened to praise and worship to keep my hopes from dipping into the well of desperation. I tried to take my mind to other places, making up lyrics to distract myself. Searching for a sign from God that David would live, I came across Jarius's story, where his 12-year-old daughter was raised from the dead by

Jesus. *Yes, a sign!* I thought. This is confirmation. She was twelve, the same age as David. This was no coincidence. God will raise him tomorrow. I closed my eyes, envisioning him regaining consciousness. It would be a victory that validates everything, I believe. "I know God can raise him from the dead! I know he can heal our son. He did it before (referring to Jarius's daughter), and He can do it again," I chanted, "but what if he doesn't?" a small thought entered. I couldn't dwell on the question, fearing it would dilute my faith and undo my previous work. "He will live and not die," I repeated over and over to drown it out. "He will live and not die."

The next day, we were called to meet with David's doctors. My husband, Matt, and I followed them silently down a few hallways, putting more distance between us and the monitor beeping and busyness. One of the doctors selects a random room, flips the switch, and gestures for us to walk in first. The room was empty except for chairs clustered around a long table in no organized fashion. No phone, dry-erase board, or projector screen like you would think it should have. The hospital had been around for decades, but this conference room looked new and unused. It appeared forgotten, as if it was only randomly selected for privacy to deliver bad news. There's no way doctors walk all this way to tell parents their kid is doing

7

well and will make it. Anticipating the bad news, my husband and I lock hands as we wait for them to close the door and settle into their seats. We usually hold hands as a sign of affection on date nights, but this handholding was a mix of *I need you, and I'm here for you.* There was a feeling of fear and encouragement, respectively, interlocked.

All the prayers from the night before, the Facebook group praying on David's behalf, and the family and friends praying in the waiting area taking up half of the atrium at the Children's Hospital in DC had all been sent up as a petition before God for this one moment. If all God needed was a mustard seed of faith, surely, we would have collectively exceeded the amount required for a miracle. The doctors sat across from us and began with David's condition upon arrival, bringing us up to speed today. Life support kept his body with us, but barely. His brain was swollen and hadn't been reducing over the two days he was there. He did not flinch or flutter an eyelash, and just as we had suspected, they called us into the room to say our battle was over, but not in the way we had hoped. Side note: I have found it challenging to put the words dead or died in the same sentence with my son. Throughout the book, I refer to this finality as "losing David" or "David passing." I prefer to use the phrase "David's service" instead of the grim word funeral. The doctors left, giving us a moment to digest the news. I don't recall either of us breaking down right then, but several moments awaited us as the shock wore off in the coming weeks.

After receiving the last report about our son, I couldn't sense my connection to God. It was as if an umbilical cord had been cut, but I couldn't focus on it. My husband and I divided tasks to process paperwork and plan his service. Still in shock, I cared for the kids and contacted people to be on the program. I sorted through pictures for the slideshow and so on. The days went quickly and slowly at the same time. The next thing I knew, we were at the service. This was not like the homegoing celebration of an elderly relative, someone who could sit and tell you about their life accomplishments, successes, mistakes, and regrets. This was not someone who could even tell you about their plans after high school. The atmosphere was somber and heavy. Looking into the eyes of David's friends and classmates as they wept was the worst moment for me. It was one thing to hug my friends, but to hug the 12, 13, and 14-year-olds as tears streamed down their faces broke me even more. These were the faces of children we went to birthday parties with, playdates, and recess. The spirit of the room was weighed down with solemnity. I could feel the eyes in the room watching my family's faces for queues of distress, waiting for one of us to melt down at any given moment.

Some sat at the ready in case it all became too much and we needed a reprieve. Initially, we did not provide much public information about what happened to David. Even at his service, we did not mention what the accident was. Some thought it was a car accident because of how sudden it was. I was sure people were filling in the blanks of our story with their imaginations, using glimpses of what they knew about us to substitute the gaps. In my mind, everyone knew it was suicide and I wondered what they were thinking of our family. Did they think we were too strict? Too sheltered? Negligent? Arrogant? Thoughts ran through my mind as if I were one in the audience watching myself. Thankfully, the thoughts were too swift to capture and dwell on then. However, they found their way back to the forefront of my mind in the days ahead and became the culprits for my sleepless nights.

As his friends greeted me, I noticed them wearing the gaming stickers being handed out. There was no way for me to make this occasion pleasant. His age and how he left us emptied me of anything light to say. I thought stickers might take the edge off, but it was just a reminder that we lost a child that day. Aunts, uncles, grandparents, and cousins were pinned with green boutonnieres to symbolize we'll get through together. Support began with the family, but the number of people who showed up to offer us condolences was overwhelming. As people settled into their seats, my husband whispered to me, "Should we say something at the end?" We both felt the need to express our gratitude to everyone who donated, traveled, sent thoughtful gifts, and helped in ways we were unaware of. We felt pain and appreciation simultaneously, which I never knew was possible. Fully aware that it's not traditional for the family to speak, we couldn't resist the urge to say, "thank you," so we broke the rule of silence.

Matt and I stood and turned to the crowd as the service ended. Up to this point, we had only hugged anyone who came up and hadn't seen the fullness of the room. It wasn't until we were in the front of the room that we realized how many friends, relatives, long-distance family, friends who are like relatives, neighbors, co-workers, and acquaintances sat in the pews and stood along the walls. Despite time and distance, they all came together to let us know they felt this loss, and they felt us. They could feel one of the threads in our community's tapestry was snipped early. The room was heavy and still as Matt gathered himself to speak first. Slow and thoughtful, he calculated his words, carefully separating grief from gratitude.

He thanked everyone for coming and showing us so much love. He kept it brief, perhaps to ensure each emotion remained in its place. Then it was my turn. Since I was a little girl, I've always tried to find a way to put a smile on someone's face, even in the worst situations.

I usually shoot from the hip with a little bit of an outline, and this was no different. Earlier in the program, people were asked to come up to share their memories of David. For various reasons, no one came to the mic. Some might have felt it would be inappropriate to make jokes at this time, so no one was more qualified to lighten the room than his mother. When it was my turn to speak, I wanted everyone to laugh a little. I shared stories about David dancing on some kid's lap during recess. The kid's mom was in the audience, recalling the innocent moment, and burst out laughing, as did everyone else. I talked about David's black-and-white way of thinking, recounting a day at the playground with a boy who wasn't sure if he was a boy or a girl. David looked at the boy and said, "Boy, you are a boy," very matter-of-factly as he swung. The boy had a moment of clarity because of David's direct nature.

I hesitated to share that story, not knowing what response I would get, but again, the crowd laughed with me, especially those who understood how cut-and-dry David's personality was. After getting a few smiles in the room, I needed to express where I stood regarding my faith. Most everyone in the room believed with us for a miracle. I saw this as a disappointment and loss not just for us but for those who prayed with us. I would be lying if I said I didn't feel a responsibility as a Believer to wave a banner of victory even though I had lost. I felt like I could lose it behind closed doors, but I better smile and wave when I got up there. While what I was about to say was genuine, I simultaneously sensed an obligation, the unspoken rules within the religion that compelled me to represent God's goodness whether I authentically thought so or not. But my arms are too weak to uphold any religious banners, my face too wet with tears for any church mask to stick. I don't have the energy to pretend I'm unbothered by losing my son because Jesus died on the cross. If my trust in God has any hope of restoration, I must start with where I truly am and build from there. I breathed and said, "When you stay ready, you don't have to get ready." A line I took from one of my favorite music artists. On the surface, these words sound shallow, but I wasn't referring to being ready for my son to pass. I had a host of dreams laid out for him yet. That week, he was supposed to begin computer coding classes with his schoolmates. We didn't even touch his dreams; I only caught a glimpse of his potential. What the crowd didn't know and what I probably didn't explain well is that about two months prior, I had been searching the scriptures for times when bad things happened to God's people. I wasn't trying to console them or make this hurt less.

I don't think that was humanly possible. My words came from previous pains, questions, and journal entries written years, months, weeks, and days before that dreadful day. Instead of emphasizing faith focused on getting what you want, seeing the outcome, and celebrating the victory, my thoughts explored, "What if God doesn't?" My question led me to Daniel 3, where King Nebuchadnezzar threw three Hebrew boys into the fire if they did not bow to the golden image he wanted them to worship. Shadrach, Meschac, and Abednego proclaimed their allegiance to God, knowing it would cost them their lives. What resonated with me isn't their willingness to die for what they believe. Instead, they acknowledged God's ability to rescue them and allowed God to choose whether or not to do so.

Most of what I have been taught focused on the former, God's ability, and less on the latter, surrendering to what He allows. Yes, God came and rescued them in the end, but they were not privy to His intentions. The uncertainty of what God would do didn't deter them from trusting Him. While I was taught to do a variety of spiritual practices that would almost twist God's arm to prevent Nebuchadnezzar from putting me in the fire, the Hebrew boys' trust was in God, not in the result. From these thoughts, I last said at David's service, "God can deliver us, but if He does not, He's still God." It was a risky move. Did I sound like I was in complete denial of my reality? I'm not sure where that landed with others, but I knew where it came from. Though I could posture myself in front of everyone to make that statement, there was still so much more I came to wrestle with.

Chapter 2

Welcome to the Club

"Suffering is having something we don't want or wanting something we don't have."
Elisabeth Elliot

I didn't ask for an invitation to this club. Upon entering, I was greeted by many gentle souls and kind faces that wore the familiar heaviness my heart had only begun to know. The membership was free and unsolicited, yet it cost me in the most unthinkable way. Oh, how I have dedicated myself to motherhood. Lending my shoulders to my children's feet for them to stand upon so they can be taller and see further than the generations before. Despite giving my flawed all, tragedy kicked down my door.

Observing Suffering

Blessed are those who mourn, which will be everyone at some point. Since Genesis 3, suffering has become part of the human experience. Suffering doesn't seem to be optional. Whether physical or psychological, we're all experiencing some degree of suffering. It chooses everyone, and yet no one has a choice. Suffering isn't prejudice or discriminatory. It happens without our asking and without our permission. It doesn't need an invitation.

Suffering tears things down. It deconstructs. It purges your mind and strips it to the bare minimum, exposing either the ugliest or most beautiful parts of ourselves. It can be an opportunity to grow, throw away, and rebuild. It can cause introspection, deep thought, and reflection. It can be the catalyst for transformation for the good or bad. It blows things up, and you have to put them back together. It can make old things new and mix bitter and sweet, like drawing closer together as a family amid a crisis.

Suffering has no minimum age requirement, and you are never maxed out. For some of us, our suffering began when we were infants being abandoned, abused, or neglected. Suffering can come with a face through the malevolence of people through lying and deception, murder, or molestation. Other times, it happens upon you, like a car accident, sickness, or sudden loss. There's no set duration. Suffering and its repercussions can last a day, a week, or a lifetime.

Some suffering is self-inflicted by being irresponsible with our time, relationships, money, and resources, making unwise decisions, not seeking counsel, etc. But not all suffering is a sign that you've done something wrong. Bad things happen to good people. This means careful, calculated, and strategic people aren't exempt from suffering either. The worst feeling is when you try your best in life and give it your all, and something devastating still happens despite your best efforts.

Suffering isn't always tangible or visible. Some people may limp or be in a wheelchair, making it obvious they may have health challenges. But there is a pain that exists beyond what meets the eye.

Psalm 34:18 The LORD is close to the broken**hearted.**

And saves those who are crushed in **spirit.**

A broken heart and a crushed spirit, invisible yet real, hidden from the public eye, yet it concerns the Lord so much that He's close to those in such condition. The battles in our souls draw the Lord's attention as the inner man is where our will is born. We need help overcoming these inner battles when they have been compromised. We battle in our souls to become who God created us to be. A battle we did not begin but is now ours to fight. Others may not see or acknowledge it, but the Lord is close. They may want you to overcome it, but the Lord is close. They may even mishandle you, but the Lord is close.

Suffering doesn't have a look. One can be well-dressed and put together yet tattered on the inside. Meanwhile, someone who is worn on the outside and does not have all of their physical needs met can be content on the inside. Jessica, a licensed counselor and co-founder of Zangi Bikes, recently took a trip where she and her team provided bikes as transportation to rural Kenyans. She told me of the beautiful people and children she met and how content they were with what they had. Then she tells me of a conversation with a Kenyan woman where she tried to explain her job as a counselor. The woman was confused. "How can Americans be depressed? You have everything?" My friend made another attempt to describe life events that make Americans depressed, but the frown-faced woman wasn't buying it. With all our needs met, how can we be unhappy? If you look good, you must feel good. You look bad; you must feel bad. There are many ways to be sad, even when you appear to have it all. I guess that's why the Bible calls it the deceitfulness of riches. (See Mark 4:19) Some suffering is invisible or perhaps only in disguise. I have learned not to go by the way one appears. You can't tell how someone is doing because they took a shower and have a nice wardrobe. The Sunday after we lost David, someone told me. "You look like you're doing good." I will censor my thoughts here, but I'm not sure how one would assume a mother who just lost her son is doing well because she smiled and said hello. I can see why people tend to isolate themselves when they are suffering. Withdrawing may be the only way to avoid being misunderstood. After Job's friends compounded his problems with their accusations, Job isolated himself and wrestled with his thoughts with the Lord privately.

Suffering and Comparison

Suffering doesn't get rationed out to each person equally. We don't all go through the same type or number of trials. It all varies. I once volunteered at an outreach event where we served food and provided clothing to anyone in need. A woman walks up to receive her bag of clothing for herself and her kids, who weren't with her at the time and starts sharing about how her son was nearly dead earlier that week. She walked me through the details of the onset of his symptoms, the medivac flight to the nearest children's hospital, and his prognosis. I listened as she expressly told me about her panic and fear, but things took a turn when she prayed. She made a declaration, and just like that, her son was healed and at home resting. She was confident he was ready to return to school the following week. I was happy her story didn't end like mine, but I will admit, when she got to the part about how they prayed and declared, a bit jaded by my personal experience, I thought, "Prayer didn't work. It was just by chance." Our conversation continued, and she asked me about myself and my kids. With my grief so fresh, I hated it when people asked me about my kids because it put me in a precarious position. If I say I have four kids, I must talk about losing David. If I don't mention him, I feel like I'm erasing him from my story as if he never existed. Because I couldn't handle erasing David, I told her about him and what happened. She looks at me with her mouth gaped open and says, "You have a bigger testimony than me." Again, I will spare you the feelings that erupted and the thoughts that accompanied them. I knew she didn't mean it the way it translated to me, but I did feel some type of way. Her comment sounded comparative. I didn't feel like losing my son was a testimony; it was a tragedy. I didn't want my life to be compared, and I didn't compare hers with mine. I wasn't in my head thinking, "Well, at least you got to keep yours." What would such bitterness benefit either of us? Though I lost my son, I can celebrate that she has hers without comparing our lives. Comparison brings about jealousy, contention, and strife. Suffering is not evenly distributed; therefore, comparing our suffering with one another is offensive and fruitless.

Suffering and Fear

"God, let me catch my breath before the next bomb goes off." I secretly ask God for a break between this loss and whatever else life has up its sleeve for me, but I know that suffering doesn't care whether I have a chance to power up or not. Suffering doesn't have a cap off. It doesn't say, "Okay, you've lost your job, broke your wrist, and can't escape this mountain of debt. Your car needs to break down, and you're all done. You've met your limit." If only there were a limit! The fact

that my life could continue to have problems made me not only afraid of the future but also afraid to get my hopes up. Suffering made all misfortune not only a possibility but a guarantee.

Suffering doesn't mean this is the end, but it does thicken the fog to see into the future. When David passed, I sketched a picture in my journal. It was a road that had ended, meeting a tree line of thick woods you couldn't see beyond them. I thought, "This is the end," because I couldn't envision a life beyond this point. It was only through allowing myself the space to heal and rest that the fog began to clear, and I could make out the silhouette of a possible vision, but when I looked ahead, I had another problem to face: fear.

Fear of the future is highly frowned upon in the Christian community. I'm not supposed to let my yesterday affect my tomorrow. I get it, but I can't just skip over the fact that I just lost a whole person. Before losing David, I was fixated on the power of prayer. Prayers for my family filled my mouth every morning and my journal every evening. Then, as if none of my prayers meant anything, my bubble of protection burst. Had I lost my car, my keys, or my wallet, I'd say not dwelling on it would be a fair piece of advice. But to ask me not to calculate my losses after being told to believe in a miracle is asking me to drink Kool-Aid. Good Christianity shouldn't mean I have to shut off my brain and only pay attention to the good. This experience made my prayers feel as though they weren't effective. I can't help but feel like the future is uncertain. *"Will I lose another child?" "How do I parent now?"* Do *I* hold on tight because my kids can be here today and gone tomorrow? Or do I hold them loosely, knowing they can be here today and gone tomorrow? *If things happen regardless of what I do, maybe I should care less.* The idea of living more detached from everyone and everything appealed to my fear of losing people and dreams.

Being locked into a memory can become a prison. Living out past suffering in the present can become a difficult stronghold to break free from because while the event is true, it did happen; it's not true that it's currently happening. I can type these words easier than it has been to embrace them. You couldn't convince me earlier that another shoe wouldn't drop. I lay awake at night, playing out the worst scenarios of who I would lose next and how I would be impacted. I wanted to let go of the fear, but it somehow comforted me, making me feel ready or prepared for when it happened. You read that right; fear brought me comfort. I'm not suggesting this is right or something to be copied, but to demonstrate that fear can make us feel safe. The morbid thoughts put me in a state of readiness. The problem is that my readiness meant depression. Constantly trying to prepare myself to lose someone meant I stayed heartbroken. How can I enjoy my kids when I'm too depressed from meditating on their demise? How can I have a goal when I'm certain that something else will bring me to my knees and interrupt my plans? I knew I needed to choose a new state of mind, but I didn't want to go from this to just being happy. It would have been inauthentic. I had to sort through the reality that life will unexpectedly suck, but in the meantime, enjoy what you can. A thought that deepens with time as I continue leaning into giving life all I have despite its unwelcome surprises. I may not be able to choose what happens to me, but I do get to choose my attitude.

Suffering and Growth

To live is to suffer; to survive is to find some meaning in the suffering- Friedrich Nietzsche.

Can any good come from suffering? It depends on what you do with it. Suffering doesn't determine your outcome; you do. The villain and the superhero have both suffered greatly. The villain desires to see others afflicted with the same pain, while the hero selflessly rescues others to keep them from feeling the pain he's felt. What we do with our pain affects others. How we choose to handle it matters. We can turn to substances and unhealthy habits, letting the bitterness of it all consume us till we drive away our friends and family. The other option is to grow through it. Suffering can deepen, strengthen, and enrich the spirit and soul. Though it is easier said than done, the point is that it can be done. You can live a meaningful life when you have survived a terrible atrocity, but I am learning that it is up to the individual to discover how. I knew as soon as David passed that there was a new meaning to be found. Not that God intended this to happen for that purpose, but I was confident that somehow this meant something, or at least I would make it mean something. Unsure of what it looks like to grow through something like this, I turned to reading books about people who had gone through difficult times and could live relatively well or even thrive. How can someone be normal after this? I needed to see it. I didn't have to go very far.

As Dr. Denise Rollins mentioned in her foreword, she was my grief coach. I had a regularly scheduled appointment with her once a week, but I read her book every night. Reading her reflections gave me the fortitude and inspiration to know that losing David wasn't a dead end. I highlighted and wrote in the margins. Each chapter was like having a friend sitting up with me in the middle of the night, conversing about the impact of our grief together. She couldn't have selected a better name for her non-profit, the Whole Heart Center. That's exactly what you get with her: her whole heart.

Being able to connect heart to heart the way she does didn't just happen. It cost her something. Her gentleness and wisdom in handling the bereaved were brought with the price of losing loved ones. Her mother, her aunt, who was like a mother, her five-month-old son, and her husband. I hate that she's had to endure so much loss, but I am thankful for the way she chose to handle it. She's taken something that had the potential to break her down, and while she took the hit and allowed herself to feel it, she did not allow it to keep her down. She is an up close and personal example that we can be heroes, not villains. We can be enriched and enrich others or become bitter and isolated. Suffering has within it a deep reflective mirror. One that you don't hold up to yourself when things are going well. Our introspection beckons us to mature spiritually. Scriptures encourage us to use our trials as an opportunity to strengthen our inner man. (See James 1:2-8, 2 Cor. 4:16, Romans 5:3-5)

Dr. Viktor Frankl, psychologist and holocaust survivor, uses the term tragic optimism, which is the ability to "creatively turn life's negative aspects into something positive and constructive." In his book, Man's Search for Meaning, Dr. Frankl quotes the Texarkana Gazette's article about a 17-year-old boy who developed quadriplegia after a diving accident. Three years after the incident, the young man, Jerry Long, hadn't let his condition define him. He could 'attend' community college using a special telephone and intercom to participate in class discussions. He would write using a mouth stick to type. Long writes to Dr. Frankl that

"I view my life as being abundant with purpose. The attitude I adopted on that fateful day has become my credo for life: I broke my neck. It didn't break me." He goes on to say, "I believe that my handicap will only enhance my ability to help others. I know that without suffering, the growth that I have achieved would have been impossible."

If we can avoid suffering, by all means, avoid it. Why suffer if you don't need to? But if the suffering is inevitable, it is encouraging to know it isn't the end. When grenades are thrown at your door, you can rebuild one small piece at a time.

Chapter 3

Expectations

Disappointment is the gap that exists between expectation and reality.

-John C. Maxwell

I met a beautiful couple, Jim and Sarah, who recently lost their nine-year-old son, Oliver, due to a stomach malformation he had had since birth. Standing in the foyer at church, they shared with me the problematic journey Oliver had had from his birth up till only five months ago when they lost him. Every day for nine years, they fought for his survival. They couldn't sleep, afraid they would lose him in the middle of the night. They had shifts between them, and sometimes, a family member or kind friend would come to let them rest. Too familiar with hospitals, medical procedures, and fighting with health insurance, Sarah joked that she should have her doctorate by now. Telling me a little about his background, Jim believed in God's existence but didn't attend church or adhere to any biblical teachings. He wasn't religious; however, much like any parent, he hoped his son would be healed. He hadn't dedicated himself to prayer and fasting about it but was open to the possibility of a miracle. After losing his son, he thought going to church would help him and Sarah with their grief. He found peace and comfort in coming to church, listening to the songs, hearing an encouraging message, and being surrounded by a community. He tells me that it was like he could see that God was with his family at every doctor's appointment, every medical emergency, and finally, until Oliver's last breath. Though I have altered some of the details to protect the identity of this family, my observation remains the

30

same, our starting points were different. Jim and Sarah didn't know much about Jesus or church customs, yet they found comfort and peace in coming to church. The good news of the gospel pricked their hearts. They weren't in a spiritual crisis because they weren't introduced to definitions of faith and trusting God till after their son had passed. On the other hand, I grew up in church and was filled with what to expect from God and what He required of me. I tried my best to adhere to what I was taught. My obedience to such teachings was supposed to guarantee His blessings. How did they find security and certainty at the same place I found insecurity and uncertainty?

Like Liam Neeson in the movie Taken, I stormed through the catalog of what I was taught, looking for culprits to avenge my son's passing. My laser focus turned towards pastors, preachers, and spiritual leaders for their emphasis on ways to receive earthly blessings. Their sermons, books, and conferences elevated my expectations, causing a greater space between me and the ground below.

On the surface, it sounds like I'm upset that I didn't get what I wanted from God as if I were a toddler having a temper tantrum over a toy their parents wouldn't give them. It's more than just getting what I want or having my way. On the inside, years of doctrines, practices, and beliefs I adhered to and have centered my and my kids' lives around all collapsed. My internal structure of God crumbled, but at the same time, I explored the idea that maybe it needed to.

Internal Structure of God

Internal: Of or situated on the inside

Structure: the arrangement of and relations between the parts or elements of something complex.

Have you ever been to a class or party where you had to reach into the bag and by feeling only you had to guess what was in the bag? You had to use your imagination. Your mind constructs an image as to what the item could be. Is it curved with a long stem? Maybe it's a spoon. Is it round, hard, and a little furry? Perhaps it's a tennis ball. Because we serve an invisible God, we build an inner construct of what God must be like. There's a parable from India I think is an accurate depiction of how we internalize the vastness of God.

There were once six blind men who stood by the roadside every day and begged from the people who passed. They had often heard of elephants, but they had never seen one, for, being blind, how could they?

It so happened one morning that an elephant was driven down the road where they stood. When they were told that the great beast was before them, they asked the driver to let him stop so that they might see him.

Of course, they could not see him with their eyes, but they thought that by touching him, they could learn just what kind of animal he was.

The first one happened to put his hand on the elephant's side. "Well, well!" he said, "now I know all about this beast. He is exactly like a wall."

The second felt only of the elephant's tusk. "My brother," he said, "you are mistaken. He is not at all like a wall. He is round and smooth and sharp. He is more like a spear than anything else."

The third happened to take hold of the elephant's trunk. "Both of you are wrong," he said. "Anybody who knows anything can see that this elephant is like a snake."

The fourth reached out his arms and grasped one of the elephant's legs. "Oh, how blind you are!" he said. "It is very plain to me that he is round and tall like a tree."

The fifth was a very tall man who chanced to take hold of the elephant's ear. "The blindest man ought to know that this beast is not like any of the things that you name," he said. "He is exactly like a huge fan."

The sixth was very blind indeed, and it was some time before he could find the elephant at all. At last, he seized the animal's tail. "O foolish fellows!" he cried. "You surely have lost your senses. This elephant is not like a wall, or a spear, or a snake, or a tree; neither is he like a fan. But any man with a particle of sense can see that he is exactly like a rope."

Then the elephant moved on, and the six blind men sat by the roadside all day and quarreled about him. Each believed that he knew just how the animal looked, and each called the others hard names because they disagreed with him. People who have eyes sometimes act foolishly.

The Blind Men and the Elephant by James Baldwin

This parable from India is often used to show that all religions are valid and equally true. The blind men attempt to learn what an elephant is, each one of them touching a different part, disagreeing on what they perceive to be the whole elephant. My purpose in sharing this parable is not to validate or equate world religions but to understand how we use our personal experiences plus the information of what others tell us to build our internal structures of God. Because we walk by faith and not sight, we feel our way through in many ways. To me, the blind men in this analogy represent the variety of beliefs within the Bible Believing community.

On the one hand, we need each other to learn and grow, but at the same time, we don't know what we don't know, so we could be deceived or manipulated and wouldn't know it. Because of this, we should guard our hearts, study, and not believe every wind of doctrine. We must weigh the words before letting them in, which can be scary for many different reasons. What if you discover you no longer believe the teachings of the church you grew up in? This means you might have to leave people who are like family. Some choose to blindly follow out of the fear that their studying and questioning would lead them astray from their faith entirely.

But God is constantly guiding us outside of the four walls of the church. There are clear moments when God has intervened in my life's affairs. Unfortunately, David wasn't one of them, but even on this side of grief, He has spoken to me in a dream and led me to intersect paths with just the right people at the right time. It wasn't the doctrines that aided me in my healing process. In other words, it wasn't just listening to the other blind men tell me about their part of the elephant but valuing and embracing the part of the elephant I could feel.

Early Expectations

I was 15 when I decided to follow Christ. I was a blank slate, trusting the voices around me describing God's character. God was being built in my mind as the more mature Believers saw Him because I didn't have much to go off of. I appreciate their time, patience, and passion for sharing their beliefs and encouraging a little sister in the Lord.

Growing up in the 7th Day Pentecostal Commandment Keeping (Holiness) denomination there was an emphasis on sin and hell. We believed the evidence of your salvation was in speaking in tongues, observing the sabbath, keeping dietary rules, and, well, there's a very long list. I had to keep a running checklist on myself because any infraction of these could mean I lost my salvation, and if a bus were to hit me, I'd go to hell. I could lose my salvation by violating one of the rules or even disobeying a spiritual leader. I was told God loved me, but I wasn't sure. My internal structure of God was that not only was he angry, but he was inconsistent. I was getting mixed signals about His love and His wrath. God seemed to have cared more about what I ate at the family cookouts than He did about me as a person. He seemed to fluctuate day to day according to my behavior. His approval was a carrot dangling by a thread in front of me, keeping me enticed but never able to grasp. I constantly felt not good enough, as if God was always unhappy with me. The picture I had of him was a big, strong man with crossed arms and a frown on his face as he looked down on a puny, incapable screw-up like me.

The terrible thing was that we were expected to evangelize and invite others because they needed to know the "truth." Oh, how I wish I could redo my high school years. (Hand on forehead emoji goes here.) To be clear, I would redo the social part of high school, not the homework. I know I hurt many of my peers by repeating what I was taught. I clobbered them with the same messages that clobbered me—confused them just as much as I was confused. I'm embarrassed by how self-righteous and judgmental I was. On the bright side, the strict doctrine kept me out of a lot of teenage-type trouble. I was groomed to be a good church patron, ensuring I showed up on time, participated when I arrived, and gave.

I'm thankful for the lessons in this leg of my spiritual journey. It taught me the value of independent studying and that there's a bigger picture to the Bible. Speaking of pictures, my internal structure has shifted from always expecting punishment and correction to always expecting blessings and favors. Here's how that happened.

Expectations of Miracles, Signs, and Wonders

I was a supervisor at a financial institution, a newlywed, a first-time mom, and a part-time student. My life as an ambitious young woman was about to slow down without my permission. One night, after a busy day of hustle and bustle, a sharp pain shot through my wrist as I squeezed the washcloth to bathe our three-month-old son in the kitchen sink. My shriek of pain alerted my husband, who came to see what was the matter. Thinking that it was just a moment of strenuous tension, he took over bathing the baby for me. That was only the beginning. Each day, symptoms were random and grew progressively worse, prohibiting me from daily life functions. I couldn't grip the steering wheel, put my seat belt on, or turn the wheel around corners. I'd wake up with swollen hands, eyelids, achy joints, and muscle weakness. One morning, my hand was so swollen we had to baste it like a chicken to get my wedding ring off. My shoulders burned when I lifted my arms to do my hair. These symptoms accumulated quickly and sent me to the doctor's office. It took three different doctor's visits and lab work to discover I had an autoimmune disease called polymyositis. According to the Mayo Clinic, Polymyositis is an uncommon inflammatory disease that causes muscle weakness affecting both sides of your body. Having this condition can make it difficult to climb stairs, rise from a seated position, lift objects, or reach overhead.

Polymyositis most commonly affects adults in their 30s, 40s, or 50s. Women are affected more often than men.

It had no cause and no cure. It wasn't till 2023 I discovered I had Lupus the whole time, but the symptoms present the same. Being only 23 at the time, polymyositis felt like a death sentence. The doctor said, "We want to put you on medication, but you can't be pregnant. Make sure you're not pregnant first, and we'll get you on something to manage the pain."

Well, wouldn't you know it turns out I was pregnant…with twins! I was elated! Never mind the fact that I had just been diagnosed with some crippling disease that I'll have for the rest of my life. I was pregnant with twins. Blinded with excitement, I didn't put the two together. I have an autoimmune disease, causing my body to go bonkers, and I'm pregnant. Somewhere in the back of my 20-something mind, I was still invincible.

I couldn't begin the medication because it would have harmed the babies, but steroids were safe during pregnancy, or so I was told. The steroids kept my symptoms at bay, but I slowly started to look like a black Mrs. Santa Claus. My cheeks were round and rosy. I had gained so much weight because of the cravings and insomnia side effects not from the pregnancy but the medication. None of that mattered. I was having two boys! Naming one child is fun, and now we get to name two. Double the fun. Should they rhyme or start with the same letter? Should they be famous duos or unique from each other? We landed on the names Jonathan and David. They were best friends in the Bible, and like every mother's hope for her kids, I wanted them to get along. About six months into the pregnancy, I have a sonogram appointment. This is my second pregnancy with the same doctor's office that delivered my firstborn, Jacob, so I am familiar with everyone. During the sonogram, the nurse and I exchanged small talk. The room gets quiet for a moment, and she says she'll be right back. She re-enters the room with another sonographer. That sonographer is also friendly as she intently looks at the screen. I can see what she's seeing because they have a TV posted up on the wall, so patients don't have to twist to watch the Sono-screen. I'm watching as she's searching for Baby Boy A. The room gradually became quiet. I just thought the little rascal was hiding behind his brother, and they would eventually find his heartbeat. Both the nurse and sonographer left, telling me the doctor would be with me shortly. The doctor enters unusually quickly, accompanied by the first sonographer. She shows him the screen, and he confirms what she and the other lady saw. I lost one of the twins. He didn't know how, but he estimated he had been gone for at least 72 hours based on the deformities. The doctor tells me that after I get dressed, I need to immediately go to a high-risk pregnancy doctor, who I will begin seeing from that point on. The doctor and his assistant both offer their condolences. They were sadder than I was. It hadn't registered. I laid back on the table after they closed the door. Placing my hand on my belly, I open my mouth to pray and ask God to bring him back. A second thought follows, "That's dumb." I sit up for a moment, trying to let this reality settle in. I get dressed and walk out the door to pick up the referral. Maybe it was me, but the whole office seemed solemn. The receptionists and clerks were all quiet. Their eyes knowingly connected with mine with pursed lips and half smiles. It was by the looks on their faces I sensed the grief they carried for me. A grief I hadn't yet felt. I took the elevator downstairs and out the door. I took my lunch break from work for this appointment, but now I have to call my boss to let him know I have lost one of my boys and am now being sent to a high-risk pregnancy doctor's office immediately. I needed the rest of the day off. Standing on the corner, I give him my update, choking back tears. "Just make it to the end of the call. Don't cry." I tell myself. I breathed through the call and managed to keep it in.

I make it to my black Durango and call my husband. All he said was, "Hey, babe." Before I could get out any words, the dam completely broke. I try to tell him between the gut punch, sobbing, and gasps of air that we lost one of our boys. After about thirty seconds, I was able to repeat what the doctor had told me. In the blink of an eye, my husband arrives at the unplanned doctor's visit. We sit holding hands, waiting quietly to be called back. The sonogram revealed that he had already begun the process of being absorbed back into my body. They could do nothing except keep a close eye on Baby Boy B, David. Since the nature of the loss was unknown, it was assumed that it was due to a possible blood clot, for which they gave me a blood thinner to inject myself with daily. After a month in the hospital and an emergency c-section, we had our healthy surviving twin, David, a month sooner than his due date.

My Chicken Little is what I called him for how tiny he was. He fought to be here, and I fought with him, but my battle for my health was far from over. After having him, I was back on the path of experimenting with medications to try to manage my symptoms, which was exhausting and fruitless. Every day, my limitations progressed, and every night, my arms were on fire, keeping me from a whole night of rest. I woke up every day with little sleep and a mix of sharp and dull aches in my joints and muscles. Our boys woke up just the opposite. Full of energy, curiosity, and vibrance, the boys would be jumping up and down on their beds in their footie pajamas or already having climbed out like little ninjas making their way to the toy box to start the day.

It was during this time, when I experienced the height of my symptoms, that I was introduced to a divine healing ministry. I watched testimonies of people who were divinely healed from debilitating diseases and near-death illnesses. Hungry for healing and thirsty for knowledge, I plunged into every teaching I could find. They quoted and interpreted scriptures in a way I had never seen before. Where did these verses come from? Why were these never taught?

Behold, I give unto you the power to tread on serpents and scorpions, and over all the power of the enemy: and nothing shall by any means hurt you. Luke 10:19 (KJV)

Verily, verily, I say unto you, He that believeth on me, the works that I do shall he do also; and greater works than these shall he do, because I go unto my Father. And whatsoever ye shall ask in my name, that will I do, that the Father may be glorified in the Son. If ye shall ask anything in my name, I will do it. John 14:12 (KJV)

For verily I say unto you, If ye have faith as a grain of mustard seed, ye shall say unto this mountain, Remove hence to yonder place; and it shall remove, and nothing shall be impossible unto you. Matthew 17:20 (KJV)

Death and life are in the power of the tongue, and those who love it will eat its fruits. Proverbs (KJV)

And these signs shall follow them that believe; In my name shall they cast out devils; they shall speak with new tongues; They shall take up serpents; and if they drink any deadly thing, it shall not hurt them; they shall lay hands on the sick, and they shall recover. Mark 16:17-18

What did all of this mean? It meant I didn't have to wait for the odds to be in my favor to receive a miracle. God gave me the power to heal others and to be healed. God gave me the authority, and if I believe, I can speak it, and it will be done in Jesus' name. It made the good news of Jesus Christ sound like great news. I could speak it, and it should happen. Not only that, but God also didn't want me broke. Say what? God wanted me to be healthy and wealthy. I spun around in my living room like a Disney princess singing "A Whole New World." This was fantastic news. God loves me, He likes me, and He wants me physically well and financially well-off with little effort on my part because faith and speaking is all it takes. I was taught terms like "declaring." The only declaration I was familiar with was the Declaration of Independence. What did it mean to declare, speak into the atmosphere, let the devil know, and remind God of His promises? It meant I didn't have to just accept my situation and that there was something Christ already provided that I could do about it. Thrilled about this new part of the elephant, so to speak, I absorbed every teaching I could find, both recent and old. I watched healing services in black and white. Deaf ears opening and blind eyes seeing. I was also introduced to grace, which I initially resisted because it sounded like permission to live recklessly and still say you're following Christ. Understanding a healthy perspective of grace took time. This was a whole new way of seeing God. I had always believed miracles could happen, but that was only according to God's sovereign will. This new teaching gave me the power and control to perform miracles, signs, and wonders because of my identity in Christ. He was in me and able to accomplish it! A new internal structure of God was being built. In light of new scriptures and teachings, He was no longer the big muscular man waiting to punish me. He was an empowering father figure who said, "Be like me!" Pain and suffering were behind me because of what Christ accomplished on the cross. Scriptures that talked about persecution were muted as the verses about all the good

I could receive made my future brighter than I ever expected. I could choose what I wanted to make happen and speak it, and it would manifest. With new expectations of healing and financial blessing, I began another leg of my spiritual journey.

The Expectation to Know

Running alongside healing and financial blessing was something called the prophetic. In the church I grew up in, to be prophetic wasn't a light matter. No one could just be prophetic. They had to be vetted by the pastor. People had titles, but you needed very special approval to be considered gifted outside of the pastor. Prophets in my old church were taken very seriously. You didn't just say something positive and call it prophetic. Usually, the whole room would grow quiet out of respect and reverence for the voice of God. No one would move as we sat to listen. There were warnings, foretelling, and encouragement. It was infrequent, and thus, the magnitude of what was being spoken was felt. Not everyone claimed to hear God making it an even more valuable experience. The prophetic I was introduced to in the new teaching was the polar opposite of this. Everyone should hear God regularly, and those of us who can tell the future or have frequent supernatural experiences are considered prophetic. In this environment, people can say an encouraging word, and if it confirms or aligns with something in your personal life, one might say, "You're prophetic." Foreknowing is highly esteemed. Who doesn't want to know what's next? Motivated by a desire to be in God's will, indecisiveness, and the fear of failing, I wanted to hear God and I expected Him to tell me the future. It was like I was a student preparing for a huge exam and expecting the teacher to tell me not only the questions that will be on the exam, but all the answers. The height of my expectation was that God would warn me if something ominous were creeping up on my family—yet another aspect of beliefs that was torn down and needed to be rebuilt. God was supposed give me a heads up about problems and provide the solution before it even happens.

In my new internal structure of God, He was supposed to tell me what was going to happen and empower me to control the situation. When neither warning nor healing happened, the years I spent cultivating my faith around these ideas withered in an instant. I do not regret having hope for my son to live. It is an appropriate response for anyone, I didn't just have hope but an illusion of control. Remember Jim and Sarah? They had no expectations of God or a biblical frame of reference for their son's healing. Attending church after their loss was a haven for them. Going to church after losing David made me lost and confused. The contrast in our stories shows that we all have different spiritual journeys and internal structures that cause us to respond differently in the face of adversity. What Jim, Sarah, and I have in common is that God loves us, and we love Him in return despite our pain. With the gaps in my understanding laying bare, it's time I consider another shift is underway.

Chapter 4

Faith Crisis

"Others wanted to trap Jesus, so they asked him to perform a miracle to show that God approved of him. But Jesus knew what they were thinking…" Luke 11:16-17 (GNT)

When David passed, I questioned the motives of my heart. Was I following Christ for the fish and the loaves? Was I testing God in my heart to see if He was who this book (the Bible) said He was? I shake myself wondering, how did my sincere conversion, which began without signs and wonders, transition to needing them to remain faithful? When did I shift from loving God because He loved me to needing proof that He loved me by giving me the "desires of my heart?" I took a magnifying glass to my own heart and what beliefs I had allowed to enter over the years.

What's the connection?

It is easy for someone to look from the outside and say, "David made a choice. I don't see how God had anything to do with this?" Yes, David made a terrible choice, but that did not negate my expectations from the beliefs I had nurtured for the last ten years. To me, God could stop David, heal David, and bring him back. God could have distracted him, told me or someone about David's headspace, or intervened somehow from when the idea was planted in his mind to end his life. I was raised believing God has all power in His hands and that our lives change through prayer. Prayer was supposed to lead me to a deeper connection with God. That deeper connection was supposed to mean I got special treatment. He shares secrets with me about how to navigate this life. My closeness to God was the key to revelation, health, and prosperity. Through prayer, He would save, protect, defend, vindicate, warn, prevent, rescue, heal. Was there anything too hard for our God? Now, suddenly, after David passes, people want to talk about choices because my ideas of "where was God" make them uncomfortable. I'm not saying they are wrong. Choices are real, and we see that in the Garden. We read about the dance between man's will and God's throughout scripture, but prayer seemed to have the ability to trump man's choices, for which we also see scriptures. Isn't that why we pray? Are we looking for God to manipulate something in our environment? Change a person's heart or mind so that relationships can be mended. Don't we ask Him to open blind eyes both literally and figuratively? We ask for the impossible but must accept that things might stay the same or worsen. To me, there is a strong connection between David's choice and God. God did not cause this to happen. However, I thought my prayers would have either prevented or intervened at some point. I thought all the Facebook prayer posts and people praying over the continents should have been amplified in the heavens.

Blame the devil, you say? I might add that Satan was doing his job pretty effectively. What I couldn't figure out was how

Satan's ability to influence my son was greater than God's power to protect and intervene. I do believe my son is a casualty of an unseen war. How does the winning team lose?

Blame the parents? I am absolutely, without question, imperfect. I'd have an easier time taking full blame if I were abusive or negligent. Because of my imperfections and weaknesses, I intentionally work on myself. It's one of the main reasons counseling and coaching appeal to me. I want to grow, develop, and improve. I apply what I learn to better myself for my family and the world around me. I give motherhood my all by reading books, talking to experienced moms, and surrounding myself with a community of women who nurture and care for their kids in profound, meaningful ways. I've tried my best to be intentional about building my family, which is what made his suicide even more devastating. I'm not an above-and-beyond mom, but I'm also not slacking. Could my average human imperfections have caused my son to feel unloved? I'm sure my parenting, the devil, and a twelve-year-old's inability to manage himself emotionally and act impulsively are all factors. Based on what I had been taught, I expected that God was stronger than all of this. To me, God was greater than this mountain of odds David was stacked against. Did I not have enough faith?

Redefining Faith

At my core, I want to align myself with God, which is why David's passing hit me so hard. It made me feel as though everything was all wrong. I needed to burn it all down and start over from scratch, beginning with definitions. I've wrestled with the term "faith." Before David's passing, I wrestled with trying to increase it, and since losing him, I'm trying to figure out exactly what it means to have faith. Is there a difference between the Biblical use of the term and how it has evolved in our Christian culture, where it is implied that because I have faith, everything will work in my favor? In my twenty-plus years of studying the Bible, I'm familiar with the stories that took place because of one's faith. How nations were changed, bodies were healed, and the dead were raised because of their faith. If faith means all will go well because I believe it will, what does it mean when it doesn't? Did I lack faith? Were there other forces at work? Was it not God's will?

Let me clarify by acknowledging there are different definitions of faith. When we say phrases like "I have faith in you" or "have faith in yourself," Merriam-Webster says that you have complete trust or confidence in someone or something. I can have this same complete trust and confidence in God. Faith also means having a strongly held belief, like Martin Luther King's faith in his vision or my mother's faith that she could do better than the projects in Baltimore. The dictionary says faith can also refer to a strongly held belief in a religious system like the Muslim or Christian faith. Faith serves a variety of purposes and can accomplish great things. Faith in our abilities and adherence to a higher power, A.K.A God, is essential to the human experience.

Hebrews 11, often referred to as the Hall of Faith, recognizes several individuals from the Old Testament for their obedience to God without having any tangible proof that He would make good on His word. They believed impossible things without collateral evidence. Hebrews 11, without a sermon, speaks to me of God's faithfulness to man and man's faithfulness to God. I'm not confused by the scriptures by themselves. So far, Merriam-Webster and The Bible are batting a thousand in the faith definitions department.

I believe there is a third meaning to faith. It is not a definition but a connotation or an unintended meaning that underlies the previous definitions. It centers more on the results God can deliver if you have faith in your faith rather than faith in God Himself. Faith is viewed more like the currency by which we seek to spend in the celestial realm in exchange for our earthly desires. Can I fast, pray, and tithe enough to add to my heavenly bank account so I have stacks of faith and can withdraw when I need something? I did all the things, but somehow, your girl was bankrupt. Does heaven let you file Chapter 7? Sounds like American capitalism mixed with the gospel. I don't doubt that God has an economy; I don't know if it operates within the structure I described above. Perhaps heaven runs on obedience to His instruction versus us picking a point and saying okay, God "do it"! I don't know, but I do know that being a follower of Christ doesn't mean I can have it all. I wanted my son to live, and it was a justifiable request. God values human life more than the best debater, politician, or apologist. Indeed, my prayer for my son to live isn't shallow and would make the top of the list of God's to-do's. So it made no sense that if God wanted him to live and I wanted him to live, why did I sit here without my computer gaming, pineapple-core-eating, would-be teenage son?

My expectations were being set by prosperity teachings that made it sound as if being a Christian meant you should receive everything you want. It comes with the idea that you must manage your degree of faith to obtain favorable outcomes. Health, wealth, prosperity, and happiness are all linked to how much I believe I can have it or not. How do you measure something you can't see? How can you tell if it's increasing or decreasing and if it's genuine or counterfeit? Faith teachings cover everything you can think of in order to help keep your faith up. I can't say whether they are right or wrong, but I will say it makes things confusing. While it is true that to obtain something, you must first believe that you can get it, the expectation is that it will happen because you believe for it. These teachings say that God is subject to the "laws" of faith; therefore, any scriptures you select from the Bible can be spoken aloud to create what you "believe for." The key to manifestation is to increase your faith or belief in it to happen. Thus, Christians become focused on measuring their faith and hyper-focused on saying the right things to ensure they do not do or say things to interrupt the powers working on their behalf. They do things to keep their faith up or increase it to manifest their desires. On the other hand, one must rebuke demons, principalities, and dark forces most of the time without any revelation. "That's a spirit" is a joke that originated in the pendulum swing, where the hyper-focus became the demonic realm. I believe there is truth between the pendulums. Somewhere on the spectrum is balance. God is able to perform the impossible, faith is required, we should be encouraged to keep believing, and there is a place to resist evil. This war is real, but sometimes I feel like I'm shadowboxing. God is real, Satan is real, but am I fighting the right fight?

The Will of God

There are a few teachers I have listened to that said you can know the will of God. The will of God is the word of God. You can know His will by reading His word. I can agree with this to some extent. The scriptures address the general will of God for His creation. The Bible tells us about God's affection for us, reminds us of who we are created to be, and gives us guidelines on how to conduct ourselves. It lays out right and wrong ways of living as it pertains to your body, your emotions, and relationships. What the Bible does not say is where my son should go to college, how to lose 15 lbs, or how to budget in a price-gauging economy. The specifics of my life are not written in the Bible. Each of our lives here on earth pans out differently than the other. There is no cookie-cutter way to do life. Life is both communal and individual. It is both universal and yet unique. It is both general and specific. Part of what I had learned in divine healing teachings was that its always God's will to heal. This general statement immediately conflicts with reality and opens up to the obvious questions. Why isn't everyone healed? My faith crisis isn't because I had questions, but because there were too many answers. The same teachers that evoked hope for me to be healed, were the same ones who confused me. While they could all agree we should be healed, blessed, and

57

highly favored, the reasons each one provided for why it wasn't manifesting were splintered. There are so many voices teaching from a variety of perspectives that I have become dizzy trying to see God through their lenses. Each of them using scriptures to back their statements. Who do I believe? Which voice do I follow? At this point, I need silence. No more voices telling me what to believe and how to believe it. I needed a sabbatical from church, from doctrine, from teaching. I need to draw closer to God for myself and examine this thing called faith. Was faith becoming an idol? Was the bible becoming a book of blessings and miracles only? Was God being gently moved from the center as His blessings slowly and gradually took His place? Was the will of God for me to get everything I want according to His riches and glory? How do I navigate the specifics of my life with general information? Was my faith really just denial in disguise?

Where does God's sovereignty come into play? If I allow myself to surrender the situation to God and say there is a possibility David might not make it, but God, I'm still in your hands; it is viewed as doubt. You're not supposed to think or say, "What if God doesn't?" The moment I entertain that thought, my faith has been polluted. Kiss your miracle goodbye and get used to that mountain being in view. I read in one of these faith-teaching books that it's always God's will to heal, but if we make a straightforward observation, we can see that not all people who pray the prayer of faith are healed. So, other teachings spawn. One of them is that you're not supposed to ask God; you're supposed to command what you want to happen because His will was made clear, and Christ already accomplished it all on the cross. Don't talk to God about your mountain; speak to your mountain about God. Sitting at David's bedside, I felt shame in wanting to consult God on this matter because I was supposed to be sure of His will. He always wants to heal. I felt shame in wanting to cry, "Abba, Father. HELP!" I sobbed anyhow, shame and all. I'm supposed to stand strong and command life back into my son's body because "by His stripes, we were healed," but my knees were too weak.

Grief made me punch drunk with waves of deep emotion, yet it sobered me spiritually. It was as if I was in a trance, and when we lost David, the magic spell I was under was broken. I came to acknowledge I was building a doctrine around me and my wants. This informal, unofficial definition of faith put me at the center. My anger towards these doctrines only grew in my grief. I felt set up as I walked through disillusionment. While it provided hope and expectation for negative circumstances to change for the better, it distorted the purpose of the cross. At one point, I thought of it like Christian witchcraft with all the superstitions of what you should and shouldn't do for things to happen. I thought that by memorizing scriptures, positively speaking, and denying the severity of my circumstances, I would see the manifestation of wealth, healing, and miracles. I became convinced that if only the world could see this healing or that miracle, then they would believe when, in reality, the people of Jesus' day had a front row seat and still denied him Faith became a term disconnected from trusting God for who He is and dissolved into a self-centered hope for a list of desires God was expected to perform.

It wasn't witnessing a miracle that drew me to the Lord when I was 15. Initially, it was the fear of hell, but over time, His loving kindness has not only been the draw, but also kept me comforted in His arms.

The LORD has appeared of old to me, *saying:*

"Yes, I have loved you with an everlasting love.

Therefore, with loving kindness, I have drawn you." Jeremiah 31:3 (NIV)

While I was making big shifts in my belief little shifts were happening simultaneously. My internal structure was changing down to its smallest detail. The Gospel was being redefined. The

Good News went from Jesus to Jazzmine, from Christ to cravings, from Messiah to me. It didn't happen overtly where I could plainly tell, but through minute modifications of the use of scripture. The words in the book remained the same, yet they continued to morph before my very eyes, every preacher having his or her own take on a single verse, giving a new shape to my image of God. Should being a Child of God make me feel entitled to a pain-free life? Or is there some combination of entitlement and strong faith that I have yet to comprehend? Is there a deeper faith? One independent of outcomes? One where I seek Him first and let things follow but I don't turn around to check whether they are following or not. Knowing God's will and knowing His character are not the same. There is no guarantee that my worst days are behind me, yet I'll still believe that He exists and is a rewarder for those who diligently seek Him. I'll surrender and let the reward be of His choosing and His timing.

Without faith, it is impossible to please God because anyone who comes to him must believe that he exists and that he rewards those who earnestly seek him. Hebrews 11:6

Faith and Favor

I grew up in a spiritual era where your faith made you a child of God, and because you are a child of God, you had special favor with Him. This favor would lend itself to special treatment in the world, i.e., promotions, being found innocent in the courtroom, and ultimately receiving things based on the merit of God's goodness. I believe in the goodness and blessing of God; however, beneath the surface of the truth of God's goodness lies the belief nothing bad should ever happen to one of God's children. The favor of God will guide me in avoiding pain and finding pleasure; anything that is pain is of the devil. Is that the role our culture has narrowed faith down to? Pain avoidant, self-seeking? The Spirit of God may not lead me to a problem or pain-free life, but can lead me to peace. When we tell people they are God's favorite and their marriage is on the rocks or their kids are going down the wrong path, what message does that send? I am not saying we aren't special to God, but special in what way? Are we defining these terms the same way God is throughout scripture so that it's consistent with our experience instead of incongruent with it? There are men and women across the globe and throughout time whose misfortune did not deter them from their faith. Perhaps they were more equipped to reconcile their reality with scripture because of their definition of faith.

There's a story about a team of traveling ministers who would pray about which locations to share the gospel. When they arrived in one city, the Spirit told them, "No, not here." Being obedient to the Spirit, they moved on to the next city. Checking in with the Lord, they were again instructed not to preach in that place. The Spirit did not give them a reason each time, just simply to move on. While in that second city, the leader of the group had a vision of a man saying, "Come to our city." Upon waking, the leader gathers his team, and with confidence, they make their way to the city God revealed to him in the dream. A few days go by, and they meet a woman whom they then convert. Her conversion was true. It was so true that the people around her didn't like it and called the authorities on the men for whatever they did that made her change. This foreign ministry team is then stripped naked, beaten, and flogged for their one conversion and then thrown into prison. With open wounds and fresh blood dripping from their weak bodies, they sing worship songs. Their singing invited the presence of God, and the prison warden begged to know more about their message. The more they spoke of their faith in Christ, the more convinced the warden was that he needed to believe them. By the end of the conversation, the warden had been converted. If you want to learn more about this ministry, they do not have a website, but you can read this story in detail in Acts 16:6-40.

According to Paul's testimony, I can be led by the Spirit to do something that puts me in a precarious predicament. Their obedience to the Spirit didn't lead them away from suffering.

Jesus, full of the Holy Spirit, left Jordan and was led by the Spirit into the wilderness, where, for forty days, he was tempted by the devil. Luke 4:1-2 (NIV) Even being full of the Spirit doesn't guarantee a problem-free life. When God leads us to do good works, we expect smooth sailing because we are Children of God. Biblically speaking, we witness men and women who are often met with strong opposition doing the will of God. I thought that faith meant the mountain would be moved or He'd take the pain away. Faith can move mountains, but sometimes the mountain isn't external but internal. Faith is an inside job. It's what makes the ministry team sing after their bodies are still pulsing from the blows of the officers.

If blessing was the reason for faith then Paul's ministry was way off base. Or if God was supposed to forewarn Paul and his team about the beating that would ensue for sharing the gospel, the world would have missed two significant conversions. Disappointments happen more frequently when the only outcome we are willing to accept is blessings.

In pondering and comparing the life of a Believer with that of a Non-Believer, I wrote in my journal:

What's the difference between the non-believer and me? They get sick, and so do we. They get fired, and so do we. They lose children, and so did I. What's the point of being a Believer if our lives look the same as theirs?

The last sentence reflects the teachings I've been mentioning throughout this chapter. How was I, a child of God, struggling financially, but people who don't adhere to the Bible are flourishing? The truth is we can attain success without acknowledging God. When I measured my blessings with those of non-believers, it was evident that faith in Christ must mean something more than material things. Faith in God means something more than what I can accomplish on my own. Salvation and heaven are something I could never attain on my own, no matter how hard I try.

When all the hype centers on the external, the distance between what I expect and what I experience grows wider. When you're told the promises of God about your health, finances, marriage, and dreams are "yes and amen," you grow angry when you're hit with a diagnosis, unexpected bills, divorce, betrayal, or traffic. Okay, a bit extreme on that last one, but you get the picture of the sort of mindset you develop. Instead of strengthening your faith, this mindset weakens your true faith. I've seen and experienced when the slightest things happen that we can't handle because we're expecting everything to be "yes and amen." The problem is I don't think we've qualified which promises we're referring to. With an emphasis on "God will give you the desires of your heart," we can very quickly intertwine the two concepts to mean, whatever I want, God says yes to it.

One definition of faith failed me not because of its overt definitions but the covert ones. Where the nuances only surfaced after failed attempts to apply it. I couldn't call things that are not as though they were, and neither could those around me. Seeing Christ, Paul, and countless others remain faithful to God amid the storms of life encourages me that faith isn't about favor and self-preservation but something eternal and far more worthwhile. Maybe true faith is less about a formula, and more about faithfulness.

Chapter 5

Giving Doubt a Purpose

Faith and doubt go hand in hand; they are complementaries.

One who never doubts will never truly believe.

-Herman Hesse

Disappointments bring doubts, but my addiction to religion wouldn't allow me to take a closer look until I had so many losses I had no other choice but to examine my beliefs. Doubting allows us to test the quality of something. I wasn't testing the quality of God's ability as much as I was testing the quality of interpretations of scripture. I was not doubting whether or not God has the ability to heal. I did not doubt His miracle-working power but questioned the notion, "It's always God's will to heal." If it is always His will and He's the greatest power there is, then what's standing in the way? The answer to this question becomes a sea of human reasoning. The other side I doubted was the interpretation of God giving us power. If I have the power, why isn't it happening? Are we defining power in the same way Christ meant it? Another slew of questions. I do not doubt that God has given us power, but I have questioned what it means. Have I been endowed with the power to heal others at will? Dozens of scriptures and questions for that thought, too. My identity consists of my beliefs; thus, it is important to me to discover the right way to believe so I can see myself rightly and build my family on a foundation of truth.

My faith has given me structure. It's how I have built my life and my family. Now, I don't know what to believe. What do I tell my kids during our morning devotions while they mourn their brother? Prior to losing David, they would lay hands on people and pray for healing. They believed in the God of their parents. I was stumped. I fumble for a perspective to share with them that isn't abrupt and causes them to ask questions I'm still searching for myself. In a moment, I tragically unlearned everything I thought I knew. I had no control, no power, at least not in the sense it was presented to me. Not only did I discover the limited reach of my so-called powers, but my kids also discovered it at the same time I did. So, my quest isn't just for me but for my children. My spirit has been crushed; my faith is on hold as I call God into question Him and his representatives in the courtroom of my mind. I'm angry, I'm fearful, and I'm hurt. I wasn't just questioning a religious practice for philosophical debate. This is my identity and worldview. What I believe makes up the whole of who I am, and now that those beliefs are in question, so am I. Who am I if He doesn't? To find out, I would need to reframe my doubts and give them a purpose.

Everything has a purpose, yes, even doubt. Doubt leads to questions; questions give me space to assess, challenge, or support my understanding, develop knowledge, and strengthen my confidence. I know doubt can be scary because our goal is to attain absolute faith and trust in God however, doubt can be a useful tool in attaining certainty. The doubt we fear most is the one that leads us to deny Christ, but even that doubt can serve the purpose of solidifying our faith without leading us to the denial of it. Lee Strobel, a self-proclaimed atheist, came to know Christ during his diligent pursuits to disprove God, Jesus, and the Bible. The collection of his research was intended to discredit Christ, ironically, he was compiling data that eventually converted him. Doubt causes us to probe for truth. Think for a moment if we never doubted. If we couldn't question anything, we become easily manipulated which some seek to take advantage of. Spiritual manipulation and abuse are a real thing, leaving behind a trail of victims whose view of God is marred, but the fear of questioning the leadership or teaching is ingrained and paralyzes them from leaving.Faith does not mean turning your brain off and blindly following. Somewhere between, doubting everything and believing everything is a space where the Holy Spirit patiently walks us into truth and light. Somewhere in between these two extremes is a place to process. I recently listened to a podcast where the pastor mentioned hosting a "Doubt Night" where he invites questions and skeptics to have a conversation. The title alone sounds forbidden, but for someone who has been sitting on their questions, there's a sigh of relief that they don't have to pretend they're on the same page as everyone else. Doubt Night gives doubt a purpose. It creates an opportunity for growth not just for the participants, but for those leading it as well. Maybe part of the reason we fear doubt is because we're afraid of the answers we might discover. What if the truth I discover means I have to make some difficult decisions? I'd rather stay happy and ignorant right here in the land of familiarity than venture into unknown territory with God. After we discover the truth we are faced with the challenge of what we will do with it. We can embrace the adventure the truth will take us on or continue to create new questions that keep us comfortably and safely right where we are. Our questions create conversations with God like Job. Much like Job, not every question will be answered or if they are it might not be in the way we wanted yet at the close of the conversation we must choose where we stand.

In high school, I questioned God's very existence and have done so on various occasions, but each time the question comes back to me, I feel increasingly solid. The next question is a lifelong journey, and that is "What is He like?" A question that all religions try to answer. He exists, check. He loves me, check. He likes me, check. Would he heal me? Would he heal my friend? Would he save my baby? If He exists, loves me, and likes me but doesn't heal me, what does that mean? How do I reconcile God's love and suffering?

Initial Doubts

From the age of 23 till the present day, I have suffered from an autoimmune disease which caused muscle weakness and joint pain so that I had the mobility of a hundred-year-old woman. This diagnosis was the catalyst for change in my pursuit of God. I needed God's healing, not just in theory but to meet me in reality. My husband and our two toddler boys needed me to be in good health. Taking a detour from my childhood church, I embarked upon a new quest in search of divine healing! Sure, we talked about God being a healer and miracle worker, but I had never heard or seen anyone ever healed in our congregation. I hadn't known of any miracles first-hand, but I needed one. Here I go, pen, paper, and Bible in hand. I was excited to learn all about activating my faith. What I discovered wasn't just about miracles; it was about God's amazing love. It wasn't just about healing my body; my soul needed healing that I wasn't even aware of. I followed teachers and preachers who had a revelation about this vibrant and luminous God. The Bible came to life with scriptures that made me feel liked and loved by God. I honestly liked Him even more, too. I wasn't raised with this version of Him. It was so foreign to me that it felt blasphemous. Initially, grace was a difficult concept for me because it was the opposite of the fire and brimstone, turn or burn God I was used to. But I immersed myself in this teaching because it offered me much more than heaven someday. I was taught that I already had my healing, and I just needed to access it. I had learned that my healing was in my own hands. I found these messages to be empowering. In the movie Bruce Almighty, I felt like Jim Carrey when he discovered God let him borrow his powers for a day. The famous 90's chorus "I got the power" rang out to me. I heard amazing testimonies about the dead being raised, legs growing out, ears opening, eyes seeing. No one had to make me evangelize this message. I was so excited about it that I started my own Bible study group and evangelism team. There were five of us. Sometimes, we would meet just to worship and read the Bible. Other times, we would put into practice what we learned and hit the streets, hospitals, and restaurants. Praying for people was exciting because sometimes, backs were healed, and pain would leave. I still dealt with pain day in and day out in my own body while others were getting relief, but I didn't let that stop me. I persisted. When you're told you can heal, but it doesn't happen, the natural course of inquiry is, why isn't it? The list of reasons for healing budded. Was it a sin? A generational curse? A wrong belief? Not speaking in enough tongues? Not surrendering, letting go, or resting in God? Not worshipping long enough? Do I need to give more? Is there a spirit of infirmity or death? Unforgiveness? Spiritual attack? For every possibility, there was a sermon sending me on what I call a witch hunt. I refused medication, which made my symptoms worsen. I don't regret those days. I became familiar with scripture passages and spent probably the most time I had ever spent in worship and prayer. Despite the aches in my body, spiritually, it was a rich time. I wasn't 100% sure of this "I've got the power and authority" teaching, but I did grow more confident in my relationship with God.

Growing Doubts

Like Dorothy in "The Wizard of Oz," my need for healing intersected with others who also needed God to move in a big way. These were the friends that comprised the Bible study group. One young lady in our group, who I'll call Stacey, asked us to pray for some pains she had been dealing with. Mind you, our small Bible study group had been meeting together for months while she was quietly enduring this pain. I think her suffering in silence was partly due to the idea that when walking by faith, you don't talk about the impact of the situation. It must have been so bad that night she broke down and finally asked us to pray. Before the prayer, she said she had been having issues with her uterus, and the doctors recommended she have it removed. She joined our quest for healing because she didn't want to have the procedure. Her dream was to get married and have children. If she gets this procedure done, her hopes of having a family the way she envisioned it would vanish. We prayed with her for God to heal her, rebuked the spirit of infirmity, and encouraged her in what God was able to do to keep her hopes up about the future she wanted. She then opened up about her healing journey. About how she had been traveling from conference to conference, following healing ministers in search of the same thing I wanted... a miracle. We didn't know how bad her condition was because she was calm. Later, one of the young men revealed he, too, needed God to move in his life. He needed the proper documents to remain in the U.S. legally, and another woman needed freedom from an addiction. With that, we locked arms, skipped down the yellow brick road, and went to see the Wizard. Obviously, I'm joking, but it had the sense that we all stood in need, and we only knew one source to handle it all. Unlike the Wizard, though, God is real and does meet our needs, but I digress.

The teaching on faith says not to speak words of negativity, which is known in the faith world as speaking death. We were so careful about what we said that I think it borders denial. This is dangerous because, as you'll soon see, it can cause us to forfeit how God could be using doctors and medicine to cure or at least manage our symptoms. Always stand on the word of God no matter what it looks like, but also use wisdom. Some people are so determined for God to do it a certain way that they refuse to get medical treatment. That was the case with my friend. She had been to the doctors, and they could operate on her, but it would require removing her uterus. She wanted to have kids, so to her, this method was not God's will for her. She felt like the operation would compromise the desires of her heart, so she stood firm and wouldn't get the surgery. She would wait for her miracle. We would notice her walking to her car bent over, holding her pelvic area. She wouldn't mention it often, but we all knew it was present. Eventually, everyone's schedules and demands of life got in the way of our ability to meet. Time went on, and unexpectedly, one of the Bible study members asked if I had seen our dear friend recently. I hadn't. He proceeded to tell me she wasn't looking so good. A well-known healer was going to be visiting a local church, and he said she planned to come and have him lay hands on her as a last resort for her healing. If she didn't see any changes that night, she was going to the hospital. I made sure I was present that night, looking for her. It had been about three years since we last saw each other. After staring at the double doors, I finally see my friend being wheeled in. She was frail and pale as ever. Both hands rested on top of her stomach, laying one over the other like a woman who was 9 months pregnant, except this wasn't a baby. It was a tumor. I couldn't believe my eyes when I saw her. She was skin and bones as if this tumor was slowly absorbing her from the inside. My friends and I stood next to her at the altar. The stage was full of scarves, teddy bears, and sweaters that visitors hoped the guest speaker would touch and pray over so they could take it back to their sick loved ones. Everyone was so eager to receive their miracle. When it was time for prayer, the evangelist spent time touching and praying over different ones. In my eyes, my friend was the one with the most obvious and urgent condition. I waved him down, feeling desperate on her behalf. The preacher comes, places a hand on her wheelchair mid-preaching, and keeps it moving. I was frustrated that he didn't spend any time with her. I am not saying she was the only one needing a miracle, but I was hurting my friend. No miracle took place that night. When she left, she was taken to the emergency room. Our mutual friend called and informed me of her location and room number. The next day, when I went to visit, she had worship music playing. She was always so thoughtful, even in her hour of despair, that she had instructed her parents to have lunch prepared for me when I arrived. Holding her hand, sitting by her bedside, she went on to tell me the doctors had been draining this tumor for hours, and it just kept refilling. They said there was nothing they could do. I prayed with her one last time. The following morning, my friend passed. Her family wasn't

Christian, and they thought she had lost her mind. Her words, not mine. Though a few others and I reached out to her family, they did not reach back to provide any funeral information. Our friend stood strong till the end.

I could accept that my healing hadn't come through easier than accepting hers didn't. She had been to so many divine healing trainings; she checked all the faith boxes, worshipped, and praised God as if she didn't have the tumor. I kept my questions at bay as I could feel them beginning to rise like the sun on the horizon. I wondered if there might have been some error in the definition of faith. What if she had gotten the surgery? I can't say what she should or shouldn't have believed. Selfishly, I think we would have her, but she wouldn't have what she wanted. Was this healing thing real? Why didn't it work for her? Had her definition of faith been different, she might not have denied medical attention. Was she strong for having an all-or-nothing stance or foolish? I wouldn't want to make such judgments about my dear friend. She was a casualty in this battle of life. One whose character I can attest was one of sincerity and love. I was able to jump back onto the bandwagon because it was the only thing that gave me a sense of power, but it wasn't without hesitation. I suppressed my questions and saw her more as a hero in the faith. Someone who trusted God to the very end. We just keep quoting the same scriptures, stepping over bodies, and marching as if we didn't see that. Or worse, come up with subsequent sermons explaining why she wasn't healed despite her valiant efforts. My heart carries on in sadness that I lost my friend, but I must continue to devote myself to the teaching, so I did.

Faith vs Denial

My friend wasn't the only one who suffered from confusing faith and denial. It was my third pregnancy. I was still experiencing symptoms of polymyositis, though not as severe. Six months into my pregnancy, I developed a terrible cough to the point where I tore a muscle in my rib cage. There wasn't much they could do while I was pregnant, so I had learned to curl up every time I coughed to ease the sharp pains till after I had her. Our daughter, Isabell, abruptly entered the world two months before her due date. After having her, I was able to see a pulmonologist. The bloodwork and lung tests revealed there was an underlying issue. The doctor proceeded to tell me what he suspected the issue was. He lists the possibilities: 1. It's cancer 2. It's autoimmune and flares up with pregnancy or 3. It is something called Sarcoidosis. Now, I need to pause to tell you that I had listened to over a dozen healing testimonies and teachings, which primed me for what I said next. "I have a fourth option," I said. "There's nothing wrong at all."

He looked at me puzzled and said, "Oh, there's definitely something wrong." With all the faith teachers backing me in my mind, I refuted him inwardly. As I reflect on that moment, I realize how ignorant I was. Here I am, sitting in the doctor's office, telling him there's nothing wrong with me. If nothing was wrong, why did I come? I left that day "standing on faith" that nothing was wrong with me, and clearly, there were lots, and I don't just mean physically.

There is a fine line between faith and denial. Moses didn't deny that the sea was before him or that Pharaoh's army was behind him. It reminds me of playing hide and seek when I was a kid. I would look for the best hiding place, usually weaving myself between clothes and toys as I sat crouched down in a closet. Hearing the door open, I could sense that I was discovered, but in my mind, if I couldn't see them, maybe they couldn't see me either. This is how I thought faith worked. Just keep your eyes closed. For every issue that came up, I just needed to squeeze my eyes tighter and hope for the problem to disappear because I refused to see it. Denial is damaging. I have watched and personally experienced situations going from bad to worse, but it wasn't because it couldn't be treated at the onset. It's because holding on to faith looked like not asking for help or declaring your experience to be untrue in light of scripture. I can be in a situation but not be defined by it. Denial, however, causes us to deny reality, maybe out of fear of what it might mean if we were to face it. We would have to deal with it. If we deal with it, it might challenge what we believe, so it's easier to ignore. Certainly, our ancestors in the faith didn't deny the obvious. Abram and Sarai even laughed about it when the angel told them what was going to happen. If anyone had any reason to stand on faith, it would probably be those who had these very clear visitations. My point here is that denial does not equate to faith, and faith is not denial. Acknowledging the mountain you face doesn't give it power over you; it just means it exists. We can't deal with what we don't acknowledge. To pretend we aren't hurting could actually be more of a delay or detriment to the progress we are after.

The Two Pregnancies

Plus, sign! It was 2018, and I was pregnant with our fourth. Excited, we told our three kids we were about to be blessed with another sibling. I told my mom, who then sent a text to the family group chat. I had received so many congratulations from aunts, uncles, and cousins. I had made an appointment for bloodwork at the 8-week mark. The blood work returns with low HCG levels. This is the hormone that indicates you are pregnant and increases in your blood the further along you are in your pregnancy. I was supposed to be at least two months pregnant, but my HCG levels were really low. The doctor gave me some reasons it could be low and said to check back in about a week. I went home, and on the way, I did what I had been told to do. A formula that I was told is that it is sure-fire and works every time. I pray, worship, declare, confess, take authority, talk to the baby, and I don't speak anything negative. I carry on as if we are still having this baby, trying to be unbothered by the results. At my next appointment, I turned off the car before heading inside. I sat in the parking garage and listened to a teaching on faith, trying to elevate my faith along with my hormones. It was like listening to the answers to a test before you take it. I was hoping that by pumping myself with the scriptures and teachings, I would change the situation. I got the blood draw and awaited the results on my patient portal. My HCG levels had decreased even more. It was clear by the third time I had this done that my levels were definitely decreasing, and it was likely by these numbers I was not pregnant. Standing in faith, I continued to pray, declare, stand on God's promises, quote scriptures, sing, and lay hands on myself. During this steady decline of hormones, I held on. The same cousins in the group chat saw me at a family function and asked how the pregnancy was going, my due date, and how far along I was. I had no answers because one of the rules of standing in faith is not to speak the facts. The confused look on my cousins' faces only reflected how conflicted and confusing the application of faith teaching is. You're told not to look at the reality of things but to say what you want it to be. I can see more clearly now how crazy I must have sounded telling them I didn't know the due date, but the baby was fine. The baby wasn't fine. I was miscarrying as we spoke. My body didn't care what my heart wanted. Finally, after trying to address this from a spiritual perspective, the process of miscarriage was officially manifesting. I began to bleed and cramp. I did all the things, even rebuking Satan, but "If this was an attack from Satan," I wondered, "how does he have access to my body?" Though questions filled my mind, I let them pass through me because you're not supposed to question. Just keep moving.

Another plus sign! Two years later, I found out I was pregnant again. Unintentionally, I had taken a different approach to this pregnancy. I was a bit discouraged from the last pregnancy. This time, my husband and I were reluctant to share the news with the kids for fear of disappointing them again. The tears they shed and the questions they had were not something we wanted to repeat. We held off from sharing the news with anyone. In some ways, it was a little superstitious thinking that we would jinx the pregnancy if we told too many people. Hushed and hopeful, I set up my initial appointment, which was a few weeks away. During the wait, I began to bleed. "Here we go again." I took a deep breath, preparing myself for the ride. I did not go into this pregnancy with my spiritual guns blazing, trying to take back what the devil stole from me. I did not rebuke, quote, or declare. I did not pump myself with sermons on faith, fear, or miracles. No worship or praise music, no battle cry, just silence. When I arrived at the doctor's office, he immediately wanted to do a sonogram due to my previous complications. The doctor said, "I have good news and bad news." The good news is that I was pregnant with twins. The bad news was that the bleeding was because I lost one of them, but the other good news was that one was still there. He began to explain that most women are pregnant with twins and lose one. They call this a vanishing or ghost twin. It's when there are twins in gestation, but one twin dies in utero and is then absorbed, becoming a pregnancy involving one baby. He said it happens often, but I just so happen to catch the process, whereas most people don't. Perhaps I was ultra-sensitive due to my history of miscarriages. Either way, I walked out of the office, happy to have a sonogram in hand. The obvious thought entered my mind: "What if I lose this one?" Because of all the spiritual effort I put into the last pregnancy, I felt less inclined to try to praise my way through it. I couldn't ignore the very real possibility that my body might reject this pregnancy. It was hard for me to get my hopes up and dream for this child. I wanted to be neutral as a way to protect myself against the possibility of another loss. So, I came to my own conclusion. I wouldn't deny my fear, nor would I give in to it. My middle space was gratitude. When the thought of losing this baby crossed my mind, I would rest my hand on my belly, close my eyes, and say, "God, I thank you for this moment." I didn't know if that moment was my last, but I would appreciate the time I had with the baby growing in my tummy. Four months into the pregnancy, we began to share the good news, and nine months later, I gave birth to child number four of our crazy crew.

What am I missing? I prayed for myself when I was diagnosed with the autoimmune disease. I prayed for my friend whose tumor took over her body and claimed her life, and I fervently prayed for our baby even after doctors determined it was a miscarriage. Were my prayers ineffective? My quiet curiosities that built up over time were louder than ever. These two pregnancies were my final straw. How is it I did all the spiritual things I was told and still lost the baby? Meanwhile, in the other pregnancy, I would say I hardly had "faith" and lived each day with some ounce of fear, yet that baby thrived? Faith was supposed to be about God, but somehow turned into believing in the religious practices themselves. Doubt was banging down my door with questions, and I had to allow myself to finally search for some answers. Were there any stories in the bible of people not getting what they prayed for? Of course, there are. Jesus is the prime example of asking God to remove the cup of suffering from Him but surrendering ultimately to the will of God. While Jesus demonstrates the epitome of one in dire need of rescue and not receiving it, there was another story that intrigued me. What I discovered was a time when someone needed God to move but didn't even ask for rescue, though they believed God was capable of it. The expression of their faith wasn't in trying to prevent a bad thing from happening but in allowing it. It's the story of Hananiah, Mishael, and Azariah. We commonly know them by their slave names, Shadrach, Meshach, and Abednego.

The chief official gave them new names: to Daniel, the name Belteshazzar; to Hananiah, Shadrach; to Mishael, Meshach; and to Azariah, Abednego. Daniel 1:7 (NIV)

Hananiah, Mishael, and Azariah were told that when you hear the music play, you are to bow down to the images and worship them. Here are the words that struck me.

16 Shadrach, Meshach, and Abednego replied to him, "King Nebuchadnezzar, we do not need to defend ourselves before you in this matter. 17 If we are thrown into the blazing furnace, the God we serve is able to deliver us from it, and he will deliver us from Your Majesty's hand. 18 But even if he does not, we want you to know, Your Majesty, that we will not serve your gods or worship the image of gold you have set up." Daniel 3:16-18 (NIV)

Faith has always been associated with the manifestation of things that meet my needs, so to see people in danger and not search for a way of escape and denying their basic need to live was an awesome expression of true faith. Can you guess which part spoke to me? It was the "BUT IF NOT" Wait. Did they just say, If God *doesn't* deliver us? Most faith teachers would consider these words to be doubtful. One might clutch their pearls with a brief gasp if you dare insinuate that God won't do something you know He has the power to do. At the threat of losing their lives, you do not see them campaign for heaven to move. To explore the thought that God might not come through for me and still trusting Him says way more than if I'm confident in only being rescued. They actually give God the space to be God, to be King, Lord, and Ruler. This is no doubt, this is total trust! When I leave the results in the Lord's hands. This is what my soul was thirsty for. Exhausted from thousands of ways I could be doing this whole faith thing wrong, I needed rest. These verses not only gave me rest from my labor in conjuring up faith but strength that I can stand in God without all the bells and whistles...even unto death. Azariah wasn't trying to save his hind parts from the flames. Mishael had something beyond the results of this realm, and Hananaiah gave me something that matched my reality and was something I could stand on. Having faith in God doesn't keep me from going into the fire.

What's astounding to me is their lack of consideration for their own lives. While my focus had been placed on "And these signs shall follow them that believe." Mark 16:17: I'm looking behind me to see what signs are following me to be evidence of my faith. They are giving up their lives as evidence of their faith. Sounds like a familiar verse: "Whoever finds their life will lose it, and whoever loses their life for my sake will find it." Matthew 10:39 (NIV) Is modern Christianity about ways to save my life or ways I can lose it? I am not saying that I shouldn't ask God to save my son or heal my body. I'm not against success or wealth.

I'm not promoting taking an oath of poverty or never having any ambitions, but when I compare their response to modern Christian teaching, I can't help but feel like I'm a little off track. What else was I misdefining or misunderstanding? I find myself

88

placing other concepts under a microscope. Was death to me the same thing as death to God? I pause to ponder that my definition of death might need refining. It wasn't just faith that needed redefining, but life and death also. Time and time again, throughout scripture, God is concerned about a death that takes place beyond losing the body.

We see God's definition of death take place in the Garden. Where God tells Adam and Eve not to eat of the tree of the knowledge of good and evil because they will certainly die. (See Genesis 2:17) Of course, you know how the story goes. They eat it, and they don't physically die, which indicates there's a death beyond flesh and bones that is more detrimental to the human race. I've heard this sermon preached dozens of times as it describes man's separation from God and segues into the good news of Christ. However, this message became more pronounced to me after experiencing death in such a jarring way. I knew all the theology around my son's passing, "He's in a better place." "He's with the Lord." Yadda yadda, the words were there, but they were empty. I wasn't ready to hear it in the early days of my mourning.

The death that took place in the Garden and what happened to David are not the same type of deaths. Jesus would remark that David is asleep. (See Luke 8:52, Luke 12:4, Matthew 9:24,

Matthew 10:28)In light of this definition, I see why these three Hebrew boys' had faith that was not attached to blessings or favor. They didn't apply the keys of the kingdom, 7 ways to manifest, or 3 things blocking your blessing. If they were modern Christians, they might be criticized for accepting their fate. This makes me wonder if what the modern Christian considers apathy is actually simple trust. We are so used to being busy in our culture that it is difficult to rest in God.

If this is how God sees death, then the way He sees life must also be different. When Christ refers to "having life more abundantly" (See John 10:10), he wasn't referring to accumulating more things that will rust, be eaten by moths, or be stolen. How we define things is powerful, perhaps that's why satan ever so slightly altered the meaning of death in the garden. He got them one degree off, and that's all it took.

"I don't understand how I could pray for my family regularly for God to be with them and this happens! I wanted God to be with my kids." I express in low tones and between sniffles to my counselor.

Leaning in, he asked me, "Where is David now?"

I replied, "He's with God."

90

"Then, did God break His promise?" He leans back with a smile from ear to ear as he watches my face calculate his words. I was in a catch-22 but in a good way. My anger and confusion melted into more tears, this time not signifying sorrow but peace and joy.

If faith, life, and death all take on a new meaning, then maybe I still have faith, and God didn't betray me after all.

Chapter 6

Broken Bridges

"Religion is a bridge to the spiritual–but the spiritual lies beyond religion. Unfortunately, in seeking the spiritual, we may become attached to the bridge rather than crossing over it."

- Remen 1999

I stand on the edge of a dry and barren cliff facing a chasm where a mountain peak with life-flowing waterfalls beckons me to the other side. In the open space between me and paradise is an old bridge made of rope and planks inviting me to cross over. It appears to have been there for centuries. I don't know who built it or if it's even been used recently, but it appears to be the only way to get from here to God or to the things I want from God. I was told this was the path to take to get to Him and receive His blessings and favor. What's beneath the bridge? I cannot tell, for it is so deep, and the bottom is not in view. With thirst and hunger in my soul for the sparkling falls and refreshing presence of God, I take my first step. I say yes to God. I acknowledge my sins and need for a savior and begin walking on the bridge. The second plank, I get baptized. The third plank, I consistently attend church. The fourth plank, I strive to rid myself of bad and sinful habits, which turned out to be an ongoing battle I fought with every plank. The fifth plank, I volunteer to help in the kitchen. The sixth plank, I evangelize. The seventh plank, I feed the homeless. The eighth plank, I pray. The ninth plank, I fast. Plank ten, I read my Bible daily. Plank eleven, memorize scripture. The twelfth plank, pay my tithes. Each plank feels like I'm getting closer to this Celestial City. The planks feel strong under my feet. I could trust these planks to get me where I was going without a shadow of a doubt, that is until there was an earthquake. The bridge swayed as the earth shook. It was the first time since being on the bridge the fear of falling had ever entered my mind. I quickly grab the ropes on either side of me, and my body tenses to keep from tumbling into oblivion.

I can hear the rocks grinding and crumbling along the edge of the cliff. I see the dust settling wherever gravity takes it. I didn't know I could experience such a thing. I realize that while the bridge might be trustworthy, this earthquake had the ability to destabilize it and me. The feeling of being vulnerable to uncertainty makes me crave God even more. Now more determined to feel a sense of relief and freedom from fear, I focus on the next plank. I can't skip any of them. They must be taken one at a time. The planks ahead were repeats of the previous ones with some variation and detail. Plank 22 told me how to pray. Plank 37 was about receiving. Plank 54 was about finances. Plank 58 knew your assignment. Just as I stepped on plank 66 about the power of my words, another big earthquake caused the bridge to tremble. My legs quiver as debris shakes off into the emptiness under me. I speak out into the air for it to cease. It stops, but I can't tell if that's because I said so or if it's by coincidence that the earthquake was done anyway. All I know is that I'm safe for the moment. The plank I was just on had loosened and dangled diagonally from one side suspended in the air. What if I had been standing on that plank? I might be dangling along with it or worse. Gathering myself and shaking off fatal images, I move forward. Looking behind me to see how far I had come, I was disappointed to discover that I wasn't as close to being finished as I thought I was. It would be quicker for me to head backward to safety than to keep going. It was like a nightmare where the bridge just kept getting longer, like a treadmill under my feet; I wasn't getting anywhere. Mid-frustration, another earthquake hits, one bigger than the first two.

I try to remember the inscriptions on the planks that told me what to do to get across safely. I hurry to employ everything I can think of as the rumble grows stronger, closer, and louder. My heart pounds as I see the ropes behind me snap, and the planks begin to fall slowly and orderly. *"This can't be happening,"* I think to myself. *"I've made it this far doing everything the planks said to do."* All assurance parts from under me as well as within me. My stomach drops, reminding me of the laws of gravity. I fall, I fall, I fall till it all turns black. With a blink, like a video game, I'm back on top of the precipice, out of breath and frantically touching my body to check that I'm in one piece. In front of me across the way is that same effervescent waterfall and gleaming presence of God and the bridge. Did someone hit the reset button? I want God, but this bridge has me shaken. Trembling with fear, I have no desire to budge as my mind explores the obvious what-ifs. What if I don't make it across? What if there's another earthquake? Was God testing me? If I did everything the planks said and earthquakes still happen, would the planks even be the right way across? Is the bridge the only way across? Each plank's job was supposed to bring me closer to God or, at the very least, stop the earthquakes, right? I'm supposed to be able to tell mountains to move and speak peace to storms. Was that literal or figurative? Were those verses inapplicable because this was an earthquake? How could this bridge be trusted if it didn't make good the last time? What would you be thinking?

I take a deep breath and muster up the courage to try it again despite my fears of being "molly whopped" by another earthquake. The first planks were as strong and sturdy as they were at first. About a third of the way through, the planks started to creek. The wobbliness triggered the drop in my stomach. As I inch onward, some planks were splintered or cracked straight down the center, waiting for my foot to finish it off and break in two.

How could something so unstable be the only way to God? If He wants me to come to Him, and I want to be there too, why did He just watch me collapse? Now, I feel bad for questioning Him and this rickety bridge. Deep into my own grumbling about how this whole thing is unfair, a small tremor sends me into immediate distress. Too afraid that the planks are too weak to run on, I freeze and squeeze my eyes tightly, hoping that history won't repeat itself. The whole bridge is broken, and I have no way to control the earthquakes. Will I ever reach the other side?

If you haven't caught it already, this is an allegory of my spiritual journey. The planks are Christian disciplines as set forth in scripture. Some are instructions given by Christ, and others are a conglomeration of sermons that extend or embellish the teachings of Christ. The earthquakes and tremors are my life events: sickness, miscarriages, financial issues, marital problems, and loss. On the other hand, God represents both God, who He really is, and my internal structure, of who I think He is. There is an expectation of earthly blessings if I put these things into practice. The bridge was supposed to be reliable in connecting me with God. So, I put my faith in this bridge till the earthquake broke it all. That is, I put my faith in all these practices till we lost David, and it felt like my religion (so to speak) was broken and useless. The earthquake leveled me.

The Church Plank

The church plank was obliterated the day we lost David. My desire to attend church was purely out of trying to get into a routine, but I lacked any genuine inclination to want to be there. Kind of like going to the gym; it's good to go, but you really don't want to. The numbness that accompanied my grief interfered with my ability to connect with the church announcements, let alone the actual sermon.

Watching the faces in the congregation, everyone around me was engaged, and I sat enraged. Did any of them feel betrayed by the preacher? Did anyone else feel let down in the aftermath of their earthquake? Were some of them pretending they were confident in the bridge while standing with a heavy distrust on the edge of the cliff like me? "Have faith," they say, but it was supposed to be by faith I could tell the troubles to go away. Simple answers won't do here. I've lost a son standing on these beliefs. I've gone to church more than half my life, and my church attendance didn't avert the tragedy that shook me. It was the church that taught me definitions of faith to mean favor, and so now I blame the church, no denomination in particular, for getting my hopes up. For not preparing me better, for gassing me up with an illusion of control.

There was no warning that bad things would happen even after you prayed. No one mentioned that saying "in the name of Jesus" doesn't prevent suffering. Were the planks about Jesus or me getting what I wanted out of life? Or was there a place for both? Were they leading me to God or His things? There weren't any planks that instructed me about what to do when storms rage on after you say cease or wars that continue after you've proclaimed peace. None of the planks mentioned that mountains might not move and what to do when they don't. I used to enjoy church, but now I'm just jaded. There was nothing anyone on the stage could say to give me back the confidence I had lost. Every word of hope or encouragement to trust the bridge again was like someone seasoning my wound with salt. "Why did I come?" I'd think to myself. When service was over, I had accumulated more ammunition so that I would not come the following week. I was spiritually paralyzed, not knowing what preacher or what practice to trust. Since I found receiving in this head space difficult, I decided to roll up my sleeves. Onward to try the next plank.

Ministry Plank

One Sunday morning, the church announcements begin to roll on the screen. I watch as the volunteer request appears with dates, times, and sign-ups. I thought to myself that volunteering would be multi-purpose; it would help me get back to doing what I love, which is helping people, and I could make connections and start to build a community for my family in our new surroundings.

I helped when and where I was needed, but something was missing. I check in with myself to see what the source of this discontentment is. It wasn't numbness or anger. It wasn't even an emotion; it was a belief. There is nothing wrong with volunteering at the local church, but what this broken bridge caused me to pay attention to is the nuances. The underlying beliefs that kept God and me in a box. I needed to start, lead, or be a part of someone's ministry to validate me as doing God's work. I pause to evaluate my ambitions, my motives, and the source of my beliefs.

Growing up in church, I was groomed to work within the ministry, which meant aligning my abilities with the needs of the church. I have always been ambitious and had the capacity to take on a lot of things at once. I busied myself with choir, children's church, youth ministry, cleaning up, setting up, taking down, coordinating outreach, leading Bible study, young adult ministry, organizing conferences, counseling, mentoring, workshops, and a host of other things. My strong work ethic and a value for community made it easy for me to busy myself with church work. I was doing God's work on the outside, but inwardly, my drive was coming from feeling like God was disappointed with me and nothing I did was ever enough.

The pats on the back motivated me, and my motives shifted from serving God to making people happy. The two became synonymous, making it difficult for me to say "no." Keeping people happy was like keeping God happy to some extent. It was as if my only way of knowing that God was pleased with me was if people gave me the nod. I had no other gauge for how well I was doing. God wasn't telling me, "Okay, Jazz. You can stop now." or "Great job, girl. Keep up the good work." My feedback on whether I should quit or keep going wasn't coming from a burning bush, so I was taking my best guess. I chased significance, love, and approval through acts of service. Was it the number of things I was doing that made God happy with me? Am I doing enough? Am I important? Was I getting more heavenly brownie points for all of this? Jesus said, "Come unto me, all ye that labor and are heavy laden, and I will give you *rest*." Matthew 11:28

Stepping on this hallowed plank made me realize I was not at rest with Him. My feelings of inadequacy, combined with messages teaching me that I needed to do more, drove me to do 1,000 things. I was trying to convince myself, God, and my community I was worthy, and this was the first time I saw this about myself. What would I be doing if I truly felt significant and loved no matter what?

I don't know, but I quit! I took myself off the sign-ups and decided to leave my schedule and heart open until I had clarity on my next thing. I needed to learn that God approves of me without running myself and my family into the ground. I'm thankful for the opportunities I was given to serve and use my talents. I appreciate the leaders who entrusted me with their parishioners and am grateful I had a place to serve.I'm even thankful for this broken plank that invoked reflection and removed static interference of wrong beliefs. I must learn to trust God in the stillness of my schedule. In time, I would come across a plank to serve again, but it would be done with intention, meaning, and peace.

Music Plank

I read familiar words on a screen, mouthed them, and hummed them to myself, but none of them penetrated my heart like they used to. I take my time to pay attention to myself and what I feel as I read the words and notice something. Any song that mentioned miracles, signs, wonders, blessings, or that God was going to give me anything good my ears heard, but my heart could not feel. I discovered a plank was broken.

Before the earthquake, I was one of the first people standing at attention when this segment of service began, ready to participate with the worship leaders. One of the ways I knew my spirit was crushed was because the songs I once enjoyed all sounded dull. This impenetrable shield repelled the chorus that used to make waves in my heart. The lyrics were a taunting, melodic reminder of my pain. I didn't want to hear how good God was, and I couldn't vouch for Him being a miracle worker or way-maker. When everyone stood for the songs, I sat in defiance, like a toddler determined to disengage and let everyone know it. I wasn't being childish, I was hurt. I needed help sorting through these complicated thoughts and emotions before I could authentically worship. I could have stood to make everyone else feel comfortable and give the appearance that I was okay, but my church mask was broken. I didn't have it in me to assimilate with the crowd for the crowd's sake. For once, I just wanted to be honest with myself and my God. I'm not feeling this.

Music plays an important role in most Christian churches, and if you aren't vibing with it, something must be wrong with you, right? We view Christian music as worship and, therefore, our way of connecting to God. Though this plank was broken, it was restored, and a new way of connecting with God emerged.

One day, while driving home with my family, I was playing a favorite gospel song of mine that used to make me bawl because it was so touching. I sang along, waiting for the familiar warmth to fill my heart and the tears to flow at any moment. Before I knew it, the song was over, and I felt a sense of guilt for not feeling anything. What happened to the match that lit my fire from this song? With my husband and kids in the car, I spoke to the Lord in my heart. "God, I don't know why I'm not connecting with these words. What's wrong with me?" Very clearly, right back in my heart, I feel the Lord speak to me, saying, "What words would *you* sing to me?" I searched my heart for words that meant something to me personally, and as genuine sentiments floated through my mind, tears silently streamed. It was as if God asked me, "Who do you say I am?" It didn't matter that I couldn't vibe with songs that got everyone else going. Christian culture aside, I discovered how often we wait for the music to lead us to worship instead of leading ourselves into it. I could sing a song and expect it to connect me to God, or I can connect to God and let my own personal words flow from there. I had discovered a new way of connecting with God that did not resemble the prescribed methods I was accustomed to. I was afraid that because I wasn't doing it the usual way, maybe my heart had grown offended and hard towards Him, but this moment revealed He wasn't in a box, and neither was I. I can enjoy other people's songs to God, but this broken plank forced a melody out of me that allowed me to express my very own reverence and acknowledgment of Him that was deeply personal. I enjoy praise and worship songs, but I no longer use my response to them as a measurement of my closeness or distance from the Lord. I now know I can have a song in the valley.

Prayer

In prayer, it is better to have a heart without words than words without a heart. "- John Bunyan.

Somehow, my mind made a distinction. God didn't fail me; prayer did. Prayer doesn't work. I didn't say it aloud; I just stopped praying as I used to. There wasn't just one, but several of these planks sprinkled throughout the bridge. I couldn't trust it...not again. I stare blankly, replaying all of my prayers in the emergency room, praying for protection over my kids at night. I'm perplexed by the fact that we lost him just after we finished devotion. For the first time in my whole spiritual journey, I questioned the purpose and meaning of prayer. Yes, I've read the books and heard the preacher, but this was my first time needing to know it in a more personal way.

Why do we pray? What's the purpose of it? What was I expecting it to do, control God? Did I think that I could put a demand on Him through prayer, and He had to perform it because of the quantity of my faith? If I can't get what I want, why pray? Sounds like a bratty, selfish question, but a real one. Perhaps revealing a selfish heart, although I don't see praying for our loved ones to live as being selfish. Mary and Martha weren't selfish in asking Jesus for His help when their brother Lazarus died, and Jesus wasn't selfish in raising him from the dead. Healing and dead rising don't seem to make the list of selfish prayer requests.

Jesus even used the example of the unjust judge to encourage us to pray.

And he spake a parable unto them to this end, that men ought always to pray, and not to faint; 2 Saying, There was in a city a judge, which feared not God, neither regarded man. 3 And there was a widow in that city; and she came unto him, saying, Avenge me of mine adversary. And he would not for a while: but afterward, he said within himself, Though I fear not God, nor regard man; Yet because this widow troubleth me, I will avenge her, lest by her continual coming she weary me. Luke 18:1-5 (KJV)

Did I not "weary" God enough? Were all those who were praying for David to live not enough wearying? If the fervent prayer of the righteous availeth much, what happened in my case? Was the problem fervency, or was there not enough righteousness?

Sure, prayer had worked before in other scenarios, but were those just coincidences? Like how the second earthquake stopped when I "told it" to. Why would God answer a prayer about a job promotion but not keep my son alive?

Maybe it is the same reason He allowed His son to heal the lepers but still sent Him through agonizing torture on the cross. Again, searching for scriptures of people who prayed and didn't receive what they asked for, I was reminded of the following verse.

39 Jesus went out as usual to the Mount of Olives, and his disciples followed him. 40 On reaching the place, he said to them, "Pray that you will not fall into temptation." 41 He withdrew about a stone's throw beyond them, knelt down, and prayed, 42 "Father, if you are willing, take this cup from me; yet not my will, but yours be done." 43 An angel from heaven appeared to him and strengthened him. 44 And being in anguish,

he prayed more earnestly, and his sweat was like drops of blood falling to the ground. Luke 22:39-44 (NIV)

I take note of what Christ said to his disciples and what happened after He Himself prayed. Instead of telling His friends to prepare for battle, He tells them to pray they don't fall into temptation. Then, when Christ prayed to be rescued from the fate of his physical torment, He wasn't delivered from it, but strengthened for it. Observing Christ's prayer I causes me to adjust my expectations and select my words carefully. As Christ instructed His disciples, I pray that I do not fall into temptation and for the cup of suffering to pass, but if it doesn't that God would give me the strength to endure.

Back to the Bridge

The bridge was useful for introspection, for me to ponder what I believe. I had an opportunity to take a step back and look at the fragments that broke, not on the bridge, but in me. I contemplate that perhaps the brokenness wasn't all bad. As I'm looking down at the bridge, trying to muster up the courage to walk across, I see a figure move in the distance. Still not having moved an inch onto the next plank, this figure made of light comes to me. It doesn't use the bridge at all and comes with nothing but itself. Its shimmering, golden hand is placed on my heart and immediately gives me peace. Despite all the planks that had been broken and my inability to move forward, it did not stop him from getting to me. Instead of answering my questions to restore the planks or bringing me success as proof it was Him, He ignored the rules I had so dedicated myself to and met me right where I was. He didn't give me more to-dos or doctrines.. He simply gave me Himself.

Chapter 7

To Feel or Not to Feel

"Feeling depressed, tryna live up to this positive image. When everything develops from the negatives."
Tobi Lou, Pray for Real

Our feelings have a place in our lives, but what we do with them can be controversial, especially in the Christian community. Christians can be some of the most emotionally confused groups of people because we're trying to shut down our feelings, figure out the will of God and follow His leading. We ignore how we feel to appear to be Christ-like, but deep down, we are resentful and bitter. Does "denying yourself" mean not trusting your gut when you feel something is off? As a Believer, I have heard messages that teach us to dismiss our feelings. Feeling lost and too afraid to make the wrong decisions and ultimately wanting to avoid disappointing God, some Believers become dependent on their pastors or others to tell them what to do because the subtle message is you can't trust yourself. We go from feeling insecure in the world to feeling insecure with God. If we're supposed to discredit everything we feel, why did God give us emotions in the first place? Is it some cruel trick to give us something we must figure out how to eliminate? Or, much like the bodies He gave us, is it something to steward over? They must all have a purpose, even if that purpose is to lead us to see our need for a Savior. When God created us, He did not say to segment the parts of Adam and Eve, itemizing each part as either good or bad. Our entire being in our original form, according to Genesis, "is good." I don't think emotions came later as part of the curse; at least, that's not what I read. What we read is a book full of stories about the people God cared for and their very human, not robotic, engagement with God. We read about laughter with Sarai and Abram, grief with Jacob, joy with the battles the Israelites won, and anger...lots of anger sprinkled throughout the Bible. We don't see God rebuking people for their negative emotions, but what we do with them. Take this conversation between God and Cain, for example:

So, Cain was very angry, and his face was downcast." Then the Lord said to Cain, "Why are you angry? Why is your face downcast?" If you do what is right, will you not be accepted? But if you do not do what is right, sin is crouching at your door; it desires to have you, but you must rule over it." Genesis 4:5-6 (NIV)

Cain's anger was an internal signal that he was jealous of his brother and out of alignment with God. God wanted to bring that to his attention by asking him a question that would make him reflect. God then showed him that he didn't need to be jealous, providing him a way to rectify the situation and warning him what would happen if he let this emotion lead. God didn't shut the door on Cain because of his offering and didn't even punish him for feeling angry and jealous. He didn't say, stop feeling like this. Instead of giving him a new way to feel, he gave him a new way to think, knowing that the feelings would follow.

God is so wise! He provides a new way of thinking and believing through Christ. Feelings follow your thoughts. This may be part of the reason we are told to take thoughts captive. Going deeper within the human soul, you would need to address one's beliefs to change their thoughts and feelings. Our beliefs and values steer us. As the Lord changes what we believe, our thoughts and feelings change, too. God never said to do away with our feelings but to live with our feelings submitted to His guidance, sort of like what we see He did with Cain. Unfortunately, Cain chose his feelings over God, which I have been guilty of more times than I'd like to admit.

Emotions are not a human defect but a part of God's intelligent design. I can hear my mentor, Mary, reminding me that our emotions don't tell the truth, but they do tell the truth about the individual. I didn't think God wanted me to feel because all of my feelings were sinful. I thought I was just supposed to be a happy Christian. Lying to myself that whole time, I became embittered, resentful, and passive-aggressive. Now, I see my emotions as telling me the truth about myself and highlighting an area in my life that might need to be transformed.

God created every part of us with a purpose, and because the enemy of our souls can only destroy what God creates, he seeks to contort, distort, and extort God's creation. He either wants us to give in fully to our emotions as our guide for life, which ultimately leads to a life of confusion, chaos, and self-destruction, or not use our emotions at all, living in a state of denial, detachment, and dysfunction. Satan's plot to twist our emotions isn't always obvious. We read so many verses about fear, anger, or jealousy, but there is an emotion that we seek after, more attractive and deceitful than the rest, one our American culture thrives on, our constitution encourages, and everyone feels entitled to, and that is happiness.

Between Cultures

The way we value happiness in this country increases our depression. The gap between what we think will make us happy and the reality of where we are creates more unhappiness. I have never been to another continent, but I assume Christianity takes on a variety of forms depending on the culture it's steeped within. This grieving process is taking me on a tour of the belief systems instilled in me by my American-Christian culture. American culture has influenced the church, creating a sub-culture for Christianity. As an African American, I have a sub-subculture experience in what is called the Black church. I'm all layered up, as you can see. Grief has created a wound so close to the bone I had no choice but to analyze my beliefs layer by layer.

Edith Weisskopf-Joelson, born in Vienna, Austria, received her doctorate in psychology and emigrated to the United States in 1939 during World War II, where she taught as a professor at several American universities. She writes in one of her papers about her observation of our culture: "To the European, it is characteristic of American culture that, again and again, one is commanded and ordered to 'be happy.' But happiness cannot be pursued; it must ensue. One must have a reason to 'be happy.' Once the reason is found, however, one becomes happy automatically. As we see, a human being is not one in pursuit of happiness but rather in search of a reason to become happy..."

I can attest to her statement. As an American, I am constantly being marketed to get things that make me happy. We have a garage and a storage space full of unused things. The glory of all the things you felt like you really needed fades, and you find yourself on the Facebook marketplace and yard sales trying to get rid of your excess and get a dollar back. I'm not anti-happiness, wealth, or nice things, but I am anti the anxiety, depression, comparison, pride, arrogance, and lack of contentment that tag along. I'm anti-false messages that say I can have it all in this life. After getting what we thought would make us happy, we discover the stress involved in maintaining it, the fear of losing it all, and the fact that we still have deeper, unmaterialistic needs for love, connection, growth, and contribution that go unmet in the shadows.

Among the various sources of depression, studies have shown that the pursuit of happiness in the U.S. "paradoxically impairs well-being." This begs the question: if being on the quest for my own happiness makes me more depressed, then what should I be in pursuit of if not to be happy? If it's not about me, then what is it about? This sounds like such a shallow question, but I had to ask myself when I realized that I would never have my own version of happiness with David gone. Existential questions were flying everywhere, but I believe scripture provided me with answers that have been staring me in the face since I said "yes" to God, but my American Christian filter blocked me from seeing what all along had been right there.

How has American culture influenced Christianity? The message of being happy within American culture has impacted what we think Christianity is here in the U.S. The Christian version of the American Dream is the victorious Christian. Different names, same concept. The American Dream is the model of American life, where one has the ideal marriage, kids, job, house, social circle, hobbies, wardrobe, diet, health, car, and, in some cases, likability. Likewise, the ideal victorious Christian has all the same things as the American Dreamers, plus Christ. Americans have status symbols, and American Christians have status symbols. Americans want it because it's available, and with enough hard work, they should have it. Christians want it because I'm the seed of Abraham by faith, and with little effort, I should have it. If the quest for happiness is not good for the mental health of the non-believer, what impact does this pursuit have on the one who believes they should only experience good? Both believe for the same blessings in life but focused on different sources.

In writing this chapter, I wanted to know if my sentiments were solely my own or if someone out there felt the same way. After dropping my daughter off at choir, I took JP to the library and randomly decided to do a quick search. I came across a book by David Platt called "Radical: Taking Back Your Faith from the American Dream." I was shocked to discover his title was exactly what this section of my chapter was about. I started listening to it right away and nodding as if he could see me encouraging him to keep speaking. Within the first chapter, I found myself challenged. His words were on par with what's been tugging on my heart. He so gracefully touched on both worlds, American and Christian, without becoming rigid, judgmental, or legalistic.

He didn't come across with the attitude that we all need to become missionaries in order to do this right, but he did share a broader perspective. He shared stories about his time with secret churches in China, seeing pregnant women searching for food in dumps, and John Wesley limiting his income to "live modestly" and giving away the excess. He gently peels the scales off of my eyes, and I find myself confronted with difficult passages of scripture that remind me of the cost of discipleship.

Christ outstretched on the cross had become a means to an end, as if His resurrection was the cheat code for my definition of success. The Bible turned into my spell book and prayer into superstition. Was I using the Bible to bypass the true cost of being a follower of Christ? Did I just want God to fulfill my version of the American Dream? What impact does the happy-seeking and victory-driven mindset have on the sufferer? While the one who suffers searches for meaning, the culture gives little space for disappointment.

Shame

I have felt this shame in moments around certain people. What I learned is not everyone knows what to do with my pain. I know God has built emotions into the human model, and I'm not afraid to allow them to run their course in His presence, even if people can't quite handle it. I have learned to give grace to those who may say or shut down how I feel.

Edith Weisskopf-Joelson wrote in another one of her papers about the *"unhealthy trends in the present-day culture of the United States, where the incurable sufferer is given very little opportunity to be proud of his suffering and to consider it ennobling rather than degrading...he is not only unhappy but also ashamed of being unhappy."*

"Be happy," you tell yourself, and then you become unhappy with the fact that you're unhappy. "Be victorious," the Christian tells herself, and then she becomes increasingly unhappy and ashamed, feeling that she's a disappointment to God. In an attempt to avoid public shame, we'll pretend to be in step with the rest of our social circle, be that church or work.

What does Edith mean when she says to be "proud of suffering?" No one is proud of what happened to them. I don't take her phrase to mean that I'm proud of the event that took place. There's no badge of honor for the accidents, malevolence, or misfortune we go through in life, but I interpret her words as focusing on the endurance of the individual to live through the unthinkable and not quit. She points to the way we govern ourselves in the aftermath. Here's an example of someone suffering with dignity:

We are afflicted in every way, but not crushed; perplexed, but not despairing; persecuted, but not forsaken; struck down, but not destroyed; always carrying about in the body the dying of Jesus, so that the life of Jesus also may be manifested in our body. For we who live are constantly being delivered over to death for Jesus' sake, so that the life of Jesus also may be manifested in our mortal flesh. 2 Corinthians 4:8-11(KJV)

Paul's rhetoric will give anyone the impression this was an overnight triumph. We read his brief sentences as if they happened in the same amount of time it took us to read them, but I imagine the transitional hours that turn midnight into the day weren't easy. Job was one such conversation recorded where we read about his transitional time, and here you are reading mine. I cried. I felt lost and confused, but I did not quit on God, and He has not quit on me.

Our options seem to be either we walk around in our feelings, constantly ruminating on the negative, or we pretend our feelings don't exist to appear happy and victorious. There is a third option. Edith talks about how we can acknowledge our tragedy and triumph, giving them equal value. When we hide our tragedy and only appear to be triumphant, we disguise the truth of our reality and rob others of the opportunity to learn from our lives. God could have saved everyone from the throne, but He didn't. He could have secretly come to earth and done all the same events but withheld all the details from us. Imagine the Bible without knowing His suffrage. Eliminate how he modeled self-denial and complete trust in God despite the humiliation. It wouldn't have connected to anyone. No one would be able to relate to His ministry. But because he let us read the hardships of his life, we have hope that we can weather the storms of life without compromising our faith.

The pressure to be happy in my American culture and to be victorious from my Christian culture is like a rushing river pushing me to either recover quickly or hide my pain or appear I have recovered quickly by hiding my pain. One day, I tried to open up to a friend about my faith crisis after losing David. With enthusiasm and a smile on her face, she sharply rebukes Satan and tells me that God hasn't given us a spirit of fear, and these thoughts are from the pits of hell, and so on and so forth. The wall I instantly put up must have been visible, so she says, "I'm sorry. I totally get what you're going through. My 80-year-old mother died six months ago, so I get it, but what you're saying is not God. I will not let the devil rob you of your joy." I'm so glad she rebuked the devil because I had no other questions, doubts, or fears from then on. I was free from the depression caused by the grief of losing my 12-year-old son, and I could move on as if he never existed. That's what my charismatic friend thinks is happening. In reality, I can't begin to share with you the words flying through my head, which I later repented of. I understood her charismatic display of shutting down the enemy, so I knew she didn't mean any harm, but at that moment, I felt hot sauce in my toes. (I was very angry.) Of course, my fears aren't from God; whose are? I wasn't possessed; I was processing. It's like a person dying in the hospital because the staff is concerned as to whether they have insurance or not. Can we tie up the insurance matters after you help me? Can we discuss doctrine after I just sit here and question and cry for a moment? When my grief met the curt culture to be happy and victorious, it made me want to stay away, and suddenly, I understood people who avoided church people. I roll my eyes at myself and sorrowfully repent for all the people I have done the same thing to.

Moments like this and the one you're about to read inspired me to create a journal so that people have a safe space to process their faith. The journal provides a free space for you to think critically and analytically about your spiritual beliefs using prompts. You don't have to pretend to uphold the doctrine but are allowed to question it, your pastor, yourself, and God. You can express what you really believe, what you don't believe, and what you want to believe but can't quite grasp. It can create meaningful, deep conversations that hopefully lead you to have a more authentic connection with God. Discuss these questions, pray, and study using multiple sources, but most importantly, follow the leading of the Holy Spirit, who will guide you into all truth.

Feeling Heavy

A few months after losing David, I attended an event with some family and friends, and I overheard someone describe me as heavy. I wasn't angry because it was true but because the reason should be obvious and understood. Let me pause here to say that grief, especially fresh grief, makes you extremely sensitive to just about everything. I acknowledge their innocent comment, but at the time, my heart was very raw. I couldn't understand why someone would even need to say such a thing when it's apparent that depression is an appropriate response to loss. It made me feel like I needed to explain myself, so I did. I went home and wrote this poem to express with light sarcasm the reason I was so "heavy."

Pardon My Eyes

Pardon My Eyes
I know they are dark
The night rubbed off on them
2 am replay
My mind is on repeat
Screams, ambulance, hospital, police, neighbors, friends,
children, baby, hugs, absence, help, move, money, marriage,
God, prayer, hope, despair, drive, papers, waiting, hugs, tears,
cold, health, children, survive, night, silence...

Ceilings stare at me, so I stare back
Pardon My eyes
For they are sleepless
My heart is a suitcase packed with memories
My thoughts are water-encased; I pour out their silent messages
on my pillowcase.
Red and puffy from palms and tissues rubbing
No makeup disguises their wear and tear
At times, I want to hide it.
Other times, I don't care.
Unalluring for a magazine cover, yet there's beauty in these
weary eyes.
These eyes have met eyes

Saw eyes for the last time

Eyes that saw life come

Eyes that saw life go

Pardon My eyes

For they do not see a full night's rest and have not for many

years

Nights of nursing

Listening to coughs, sneezes, and nightmares, sitting on the

edge of the bed, poised at the ready

Might tonight I get to bury my head in a dream to escape, but

for a moment, the burden life has given me.

To visit a place where my insides are not so tied, my thoughts

are not so wound and my spirit not so bound.

Till I wake and sob again...

Pardon my eyes

For they do not sparkle or entice but rather invite fellow

sufferers

Every circle, a ring of refinement

Stripes with stories

Heavy and sunken

No memory foam eliminates the memories formed.

Rest is not assured because of bed and blanket, but as the days

go by and my own light grows dim, one day, I'll sleep forever

Till then...

Pardon my eyes.

Dark clouds weren't just over me; I carried them on my shoulders. It weighed down my posture and darkened my countenance. The indentations under my eyes and the lack of energy in my voice were dead giveaways that I wasn't the same Jazzmine everyone once knew. I wasn't upbeat and cheerful. I was depressed. Prior to losing David, I was naive to the ways I was programmed to think and feel by my American-Christian culture. It wasn't till experiencing my own trauma, anxiety, and depression that my perspective shifted for those who struggle with these things consistently. As a kid, I was taught that depression was a spirit and, as such, needed to be cast out, prayed away, fasted out, shouted out, and baptized out. I heard someone say if you're depressed, it's because you're not praying enough. This piles on shame, guilt, and depression. Then, they told them they were not supposed to look back or be a victim. So now, they're not even supposed to remember the event as if coming to Christ means you get a new memory. Could you imagine if all of our memories were wiped? Eliminating all the bad memories isn't good for us either, or we would just be more likely to walk right back into unhealthy relationships, forgetting the lessons we learned from the previous negative experience. We shame the people for "looking back" like Lot's wife or not embracing that they are a "new creature in Christ, old things are passed away." These catchy phrases and inspirational messages keep hope alive in people, and for that, I am thankful, but I also appreciate the practical application. How does someone "not look back?" The Bible gives us a good "why" but sometimes lacks the "how?" My personal theory is that we don't all receive the same "how" because we're supposed to lean on God's unique, specific instructions for us individually. Some things are universal, and others are personal things. Forgiveness is universal; whether or not to let that person back into your life is an individual matter. What works for me may not work for you. There is no clear-cut way to work through grief. You can't speed it up. You can distract yourself, but that's not speeding it up. It'll just be there waiting for you to acknowledge it.

Exhaustion

JP, our fourth child, was born in November 2020 with a cleft lip. In March 2021, at four months old, they had cut and sewn together his nose to make it symmetrical and brought skin down to close the cleft gap. My stomach dropped when we walked in to see him after the procedure. His face was blue, purple, and green. His nose and mouth were bruised and swollen like he had been in a boxing match. Trying to nurse an infant whose nose and mouth were gauzed and guarded by a metal bar was challenging. We had to keep his arms in splints so he couldn't bend his arms and hit himself in the face. Every once in a while, the clever baby would eventually shimmy the splint off and hit himself. It still makes me shiver when I think about the pain his little body endured. Those were treacherous days. Following JP's surgery in March, my husband had surgery in April, and my mother had surgery in May.

Lacking sleep and sanity, I did my best with homeschooling our other three kiddos, running my life coaching business, and packing for our upcoming move in August. My house was organized but crowded between boxes, JP's baby swing, a playpen, and toys. I ran on fumes daily, trying to keep up with life's demands. This is the type of tiredness that fills my heart. Giving of myself for my family. My arms were full, but so was my heart. I could keep up with all the plates in the air until one morning in June, in the middle of my hustle and bustle, we lost our Davey-Crocket without a warning or a sign.

Reflecting on the back-to-back events of 2021, I'm amazed I didn't have a breakdown sooner, but one was on the way to make up for lost time.

Shock [shock]

1. a sudden disturbance of mental equilibrium

We couldn't bring ourselves back to our house, so my in-laws graciously opened their home to us till we could gather ourselves and figure out our next steps. Time is a blur, so I don't know when this happened, but at some point in the days following David's service, there was no more distraction in my way. What's there to talk about after this? I wasn't sure what to do with myself. No more papers to sign, no more waiting in expectant anticipation of what's next, no routine to return to since we weren't home, nothing but a gap between Jacob and Izzy. A gap that could never be refilled or replaced by anything ever. That night, my mind was shocked as it realized the reality that David was gone. The television was playing in the background, and noise was going on around me, yet in my soul, everything fell quiet. I heard nothing and felt empty, and that's when it happened.

Like a sudden attack, I had a mental meltdown, which I can now identify as such, but at the time, I didn't know I was even capable of it. I heard the phrase, "I nearly lost my mind." Up to this point, I thought it was only a dramatic expression, but I discovered from firsthand experience that the human spirit is fragile and can only take so much before it wants to shut down. Though it took a lot to get there, I finally met my capacity. I didn't yell, scream, or sob. I didn't make a sound; I just lay on the cool floor. I found a strange comfort in it. My mind was empty, my senses had taken over, and the floor felt good to me, so when my husband asked me, "What are you doing?" I thought it was obvious that I was resting on the floor. Of course, he didn't mean it literally. He meant "what's wrong?" I couldn't explain it then and still can't, but I was drawn to the floor. When the police came to my house in response to my 911 call, I fell to the floor. When I was in the hallway at the hospital, I fell to the floor. Now, here I am, finding comfort on the floor yet again. Seeing me on the dining room floor, my husband begins to grow concerned. He could tell something wasn't right. "I just need to lay down," I told him. He asked me to go upstairs to lie down, but I couldn't get myself up. I felt faint. I wanted him and the world to leave me there. It made me feel calm, peaceful, and relaxed. I had no explanation for it. I had no reasoning or logic. Perhaps that was the inside of me saying, "I want to die. I want to be with David." My spirit was broken and shattered, and I couldn't put words to what I was feeling because even my thoughts escaped me. After he got me off the floor and made me sit in a chair, I had the most peculiar experience ever. I suddenly had the strongest urge to take my life. It weighed on me like a cloak.

A feeling that surged through my body so strong I had brief visions about ways I could just end it all. It wasn't just an idea, it was coursing through me, tempting me, calling me to alleviate this pain. Everything went black, and my body went limp. With much excitement and commotion, Matt carries me upstairs, and I'm now on what I can identify as a suicide watch by my sister-in-law. It was a self-imposed suicide watch. I didn't trust myself or this feeling that came over me. I had enough sense to know I shouldn't be left alone. It was an hour of complete disconnect and detachment from this world and everyone I loved. The intensity made me forget the impact my death would have on my kids, especially on the heels of losing David in such a way. Is this how David felt? As if his life didn't matter? I wondered as I felt so close to the door of doing the deed myself. What is all of this? I've never needed anxiety medication, but I'm not sure what would have happened had I not had my husband, my sister-in-law, and those pills to help me handle the sudden realization of what just happened.

Anx·i·e·ty/aNGˈzīədē/

noun

1. a feeling of worry, nervousness, or unease, typically about an imminent event or something with an uncertain outcome:

This was my first-time experiencing anxiety as a result of a traumatic experience. I have a new level of compassion for those suffering from anxiety, trauma, depression, and grief. I can see why Christians can be so irritating. We can be rigid, insensitive, and dismissive to the depth of pain someone is experiencing because we don't understand it or over-spiritualize it, not meeting the person where they are because we're trying to "call them higher." Before this, I never knew what someone meant by "I have anxiety." I have had two anxiety attacks in the past, but nothing like this. Now that my protective layer burst and I realized that God would allow tragedy to strike my family, nothing felt safe...not even God. I was told to pray for protection, and since my prayer for that was ineffective, I didn't see a point in praying about my anxiety and fear. My logic was *that if God didn't save David, which was the most important thing, then what would make me think He'd respond to anything else? If human life doesn't matter to God, then what does?*

Visions of losing my other kids filled my mind throughout the night. I worried about what was going through their minds when their doors were closed. I worried that JP would stop breathing in the middle of the night. I could spiritualize this and say that the devil is tormenting me, but I don't think it was the devil as much as it was me walking through the disillusionment of what I thought being a Christian meant. Prayer had lost its magic. The truth is that people are praying and still have their problems.

Irritated

When you are hurting, you are easily irritated, or at least I was. Church was supposed to be the place I would find healing, but in this condition, I was... you guessed it, irritated! If one more happy face took the stage and talked about how the Holy Spirit got them a good parking space or their favorite football team to win in Jesus' name, I was ready to toss a flip-flop at the speaker. There were a few times I came close.

I was invited to attend a conference. It was beautifully decorated, and the food and presentation were on point. Not wanting to be noticed, I sat in the back and mingled minimally compared to my usual extroverted self. As the speaker begins to share her message, I grow irritated. Her light and fluffy message was offensive to my hurting soul, and I found myself upset on behalf of the other women who might also be suffering from real-life issues and not because they found out their 401(k) payout was less than they expected. To be fair, I recognize that my frustration with her had more to do with my grief than her message. I was in a critical mood. I took a few deep breaths, appreciated the effort of the organizers, and told myself I didn't need to go to any more events till I've processed my grief. Well, then, I got invited to another event. I attend. Again, not wanting to be bothered, I sat all the way in the back. Nicely decorated, with delicious food and warm smiles. So far, so good. As the evening unfolds and the mic is shared one woman after another, here goes my irritation flaring up. I couldn't see the goal of coming together. We weren't encouraged to connect with one another, none of our issues were addressed, and the women were too polished and concerned with what others might think of them if they really opened up that they all just wore their church masks. My assumption was that they felt like real stories were too messy for the church environment. Vague testimonies were shared, giving only the highlights as if they were in gut-wrenching, soul-crushing pain one moment, and God took it all away the next. Here I go, slowly turning into a she-hulk burning up on the inside, knowing that they skipped a ton of details. Testimonies like these make sufferers feel like lepers.

Don't they know that most things are a process? Don't they see they are speaking to a group of women who are trying their best to remain in the presence of God and STILL haven't received

134

anything? I couldn't handle the facade. *I came out all this way, out of my cave, to hang with Barbie dolls.* I thought to myself and then repented for the remainder of my thoughts the entire ride home. I could have gone out to eat with a few friends and shared some real feelings. I left telling myself that's it, I'm not going to another one of these events. I think we all glean the most from those who are transparent. We connect and see ourselves in each other's stories and find hope in our authenticity. I only preserve my pride and withhold your hope when I pretend "I'm good."

Apathy

On one hand, I ran to God, desperate for connection, peace of mind, and comfort. On the other hand, the Bible, church, and spiritual practices were confusing. I am passionate about the former and apathetic about the latter. Being in this weird middle space where things are being redefined and my internal structure of God is shifting, I became unconcerned with the planks on the bridge. How could I be passionate about something I don't understand? Before I can run in any direction, I have to at least have clarity about what I'm running towards. I have plenty to run from, but what am I running to? God is so big that I knew I could run to Him for peace and comfort; it was the other stuff I wasn't so sure of. Would he protect my kids? Being indifferent was my attempt at being neutral. It was like I pushed pause to get my bearings. Where am I, and where am I going? If you ever see someone in meh-mood, they are probably trying to recalibrate. They are stuck in a part of their process. They have tons of questions that people haven't been able to answer, so their best is to be a sort of Christian agnostic, where they believe in Christ but are uncertain about anything beyond that. They believe in a God vaguely because they find it difficult to be certain of anything about Him. This is a perfect picture of me. Sure, I know the attributes of God, but remember that my internal structure of God was for miracles, health, and wealth. So, when that didn't happen, my thought was, "I can't know anything for certain about God. He's too big," and apathy set in. I wasn't hot, actively seeking God. I wasn't cold, denying Him, but you might say I was lukewarm. Lacking passion for life or anything for that matter. Feeling like all is pointless, hopeless, and useless. What seems to make apathy dissipate is meaning. Even as I wrote this book, apathy stopped in for a visit and asked, "What's the use? Your book won't matter in a sea of other voices talking about the same thing." But by attaching meaning to this book, I make it matter. It matters to me because it is something I need to give to the world before I leave it. May it be a gem or treasure to the one who finds it comforting in their time of trouble knowing they are not the only ones dazed by life's unexpected turns and yet still holding on to God in the midst of it.

Cynical

I had become distrustful of some preachers, wondering if they really understood, cared for, and loved people or the platform. This was not the best attitude to have, especially in front of the kids. I disliked my apathy and cynicism. I was supposed to be a role model for them, but I felt like I was standing on nothing. What frustrated me was that I was standing on what preachers told me. I believed them and, therefore, felt a sense of betrayal. I trusted them, and my kids trusted me. I was miseducated; therefore, I miseducated my kids. My kids have held onto their faith stronger than I would have imagined, probably because they didn't have years of Pentecostal, charismatic, evangelical teachings to comb through. I grew up with the church being the epicenter and main event of the Christian lifestyle, but the church just didn't feel like it had the answers anymore.

Gratitude

Counting one thousand gifts means counting the hard things-otherwise I've miscounted   -Ann Voskamp.

This is the one emotion you are permitted to have as a Believer. Christians sigh with relief that they don't have to do any work to try to pull you into the bright side when you start saying what you're thankful for because it's in step with being victorious, but my gratitude is genuine. When people tried to make me "look on the bright side," I bristled. They weren't wrong for trying to encourage me toward the light, but it's the phrases like "at least you have other children" or "people make choices, right?" that made their support not only ineffective but offensive. It's these moments I have to see beyond their words and into their heart to know they mean well. There were far more people who said the right things than there were those who said the wrong things, and for all these voices speaking into my life, I am thankful. I'm thankful for the reminder to be thankful through a book by Ann Voskamp called "One Thousand Gifts." Having suffered through her own traumatic loss, she is challenged to find one thousand things to be thankful for. Feeling seen and understood by Ann, I took on her challenge. There isn't a deadline, but every day, you must add to your list till you get to one thousand. Here are a few from my gratitude journal.

33. Apple Cider Donuts

47. Deep sobs-Snot cry

57. Popcorn

62. Dried up worm on the sidewalk-ugly beautiful

64. Honest teenager

68. Indoor plumbing

74. Laurie's Hug and listening ear

87. Matt picking me up and letting me vent. NOT fixing it and getting donuts!

105. Niece-Naomi's smile

113. Izzy's laugh

122. Instacart

156. Coffee and biscotti

179. JP nestling in my lap for books

228. Insecurities that remind me of who I am-human, weak, frail, limited, and finite

Since the gravity of grief naturally weighed me down, this simple practice refocused my attention as I searched for things to be worthy of noting in my gratitude journal. It gave me a break from the incessant thoughts about what's wrong in this world and sent my mind on a scavenger hunt for gratitude.

Permission to Feel

As I write this book, it hasn't been a complete three years since his passing, but the victorious-Christian plagues me, making me think something is wrong with me. I hadn't known many preachers to speak about loss and grief unless it was at a funeral. We address trauma by saying to let go of it when it's not something I'm holding on to. We tell depressed people to think happy thoughts when it's not so easy. So, this is all new to me. I searched for validation in scripture. Something that would say God has seen patients like me before. I found the following passages.

Jacob, also known as Israel, was lied to by his sons. They told him that Joseph, his favorite son, was killed by a vicious animal, though in truth, they had sold him into slavery. His reaction doesn't fit the victorious Christian model.

"All his sons and daughters came to comfort him, but he refused to be comforted. "No," he said, "I will continue to mourn until I join my son in the grave." So, his father wept for him. Gen. 37:35 (NIV)

Jacob expressed the exact sentiments I had that night on the floor. I hate that Jacob's sons put him through such agonizing torment to make him think Joseph died. How cruel! With so much anti-emotions teaching, it helped me see that our patriarch mourned and refused comfort for his son. I know it sounds odd that I would need a verse to validate my grief, but I have received messages my whole life about what strength looks like from my Black community, what victory looks like as a Christian, and what success is as an American. Losing David went against all three. Not one of my cultures told me how to grieve or that it was even okay, so I had to discover it for myself.

I don't write about permission to feel just for the bereaved but for those challenged by life. I write for people who feel like emotional lepers, shunned and shamed if they express their pain. In the same way, it is said that faith isn't a feeling; I would say that emotionlessness isn't faith. I am certain that my identity in Christ is not predicated upon how flint faced I can be. My face may be wet with tears on the outside, but on the inside, I am strong, victorious, and successful (not in the American way) because Christ abides in me. It is a weird middle-space. I am weak and frail but confident that God is with me even though my life is upside down.

141

Chapter 8

Power to Choose

Everything can be taken from a man, but one thing: the last of the human freedoms- to choose one's attitude in any given set of circumstances to choose one's own way.

Viktor Frankl, Psychologist and Holocaust Survivor

"Dead end." I sketched a picture of a dead-end sign backed by bushes and a jumble of trees on our way to our first family counseling session. The words and childlike art were the best I could do to get my feelings on paper. I didn't see how my life could possibly go on after what just happened. My mind blocked any imagination of the future, good or bad. My life was going till it just stopped. Being only able to feel the end and see the present darkness without a glimpse of hope for the future is what made me afraid to be left alone with my thoughts. My mind would go to solutions that would only create more pain in the ones I love. How does one survive something like this? How do people overcome the nightmares and triggers, the anxiety, fear of the future, and frustration with church people like me who offered band-aid solutions to their gunshot wounds? How do marriages last through something like this? My pen continued to scratch the notepad from the Children's Hospital we had received the week before. I wanted to sketch a path, but there wasn't one. I would have to choose to walk through the jungle, one step at a time, chopping down branches as I go into the unknown.

"What do you want to do with this, God?" I asked in my heart.

"What do *you* want to do with it?" came a response.

"What do *I* want to do with this?" As if God had insulted me.

What do I do with this? I repeated to myself and scoffed.

"*I* didn't cause this situation; therefore, *I* shouldn't be responsible for fixing it. You're God, aren't You responsible for turning this around? This isn't my fault. This situation took me totally by surprise. Why should I have to be the one to figure out what to do with this? What *could* I do with this? I didn't have anything to do with why I was in this predicament, so what choices could I possibly make to get me out? And what does get out even look like? Getting out of it to me was either David joined me or I joined David. There's no other way through."

As the days went on, a truth gradually unfolded. God wasn't going to deliver me from the effects of trauma or my grief; I had to choose what to do with myself. While He provided friends and resources, he left the options of what to do with it all up to me. He didn't even deliver me from the thoughts of suicide. Deliverance, to me, was an immediate rescue from someone outside of myself. It was an instantaneous rectification of a situation. To deliver meant God would set me free from anything negative or uncomfortable. I was under the illusion that God would keep Christians from doing heinous things. I knew I was capable of sin, but now it felt like the guardrails were off. I could do evil things, and God wasn't going to stop me; I had to choose what was right, which, of course, is the point of free will. These were conscious decisions I had to make. I had never been to the bottom of myself like this before. For the first time, without the cushion of church, worship music, or preaching, I was left to my own devices. I hit the rawness of just myself and God, nothing standing between us. Nothing softened the blows of terrible choices I could make in this situation. I had the power...to choose terribly or choose well. This felt like freedom, but not the good kind. Freedom to do all sorts of things. I had had it all along, but this was the first time I really felt that freedom. I knew I had it in theory, but since all theories were being challenged at this point, I understood my power to choose in a new way. After having that complete meltdown, I felt all the wrong choices begging me to pick them. Afraid of my own ability to mess things up, I clung to God even more.

I take a deep breath and begin to take a walk. No parent should have to walk. I walk under the archway, passing names and dates and making my way to David's unmarked site. I stand there holding flowers and a heart full of conversation to be had with him and God. "David, I can't be with you yet. It is not my time. I still have your brothers and sister to raise. God hasn't

145

called me to be with you at this time, but there will come a day when we can be together, but I can't join you now." I place the flowers down after making my decree to David. I look up to the sky, honoring my Creator. I breathe in His air in my lungs, and with His air, I speak, "I choose life."

Returning home after my little ceremony, I sat on the edge of my bed and asked God, "What now?"

"Heal and rest." His words relaxed my soul and restored a little hope that I could heal and be okay.

It was then I leaned into the process of healing and resting by making one small conscious choice at a time. Drinking water, taking vitamins, making my bed, and going for a walk were some simple physical decisions I had to make. What about prayer and devotion, you ask? It's in there when I'm drinking water, making my bed, or going for a walk. Much like the old song says, "I need thee every hour." If my lips weren't moving, my heart was doing the talking, and it wasn't always flowery, neat prayers I would repeat in a devotional book. Although, those can be helpful when you're lost for words.

Choices seem small, but within them is our power and authority to mold our identity and meaning. Replaying His question "What do you want to do with this?" felt like God was parenting me through a teachable moment. This is about more than just my ability to cope. I am about to learn deeper lessons about me, God, and the world.

Chapter 9
Integrating Not Resolving Grief

"Prayer is my weapon; therapy is my strategy."
-Dr. Anita Phillip addressing the powerful combination of faith
and therapy.

Thirty former prisoners of war from the Hanoi Hilton camp in Vietnam were asked how they were able to endure 6-8 years of imprisonment where they were tortured and held in solitary confinement, and yet they came out living successful, meaningful lives. How were they able to withstand these conditions for so long? The answer is "tap code." The prisoners had developed a code by tapping out the alphabet as a means to communicate with one another. "They were never isolated and could still support each other. 'Everybody needs a tap code to get through tough times. Very few can go it alone.'" Resilient Grieving by Lucy Hone

Difficult things become a little more bearable when there's company. I understand that no one can walk in my shoes and take this burden from me, but God has provided me with people to help me heal along the way. Recovering from trauma, learning how to integrate grief, and adjusting to David's absence was multifaceted. I didn't want to get stuck interpreting my present through the lens of my past, so I set my intentions to find resources to pull me through, like counseling, Grief Share, prayer, writing, and meditation. When thoughts of "I'm alone" tried to consume me, I remembered a long list of people who had tapped in with us.

One of the first people to tap-in was one of our dearest friends, Ryan Bastress, a full-time traveling minister who put his life and ministry on hold to be with us from start to finish. He drove me from the local hospital to meet up with Matt, who was being Medevacked with David, at the children's hospital in DC. He and his wife worked together and covered all of our bases, from accepting phone calls, praying with us, fielding questions, meeting with doctors, organizing and preaching at David's service, boxing up, and moving us from Maryland to Pennsylvania. The list goes on and on. They even held onto David's belongings in their garage till I was ready to pick them up, and then they stayed with me in case I needed emotional support as I went through his things. We are blessed to call him a friend.

Some people tapped in who I hadn't seen or engaged with in years. News of David's passing spread quickly with the use of a Facebook Group titled David's Prayer Group Ryan made within hours of learning about David's condition. It didn't take long before family and the community of friends began responding by sending flowers and cards once the final pronouncement was made. One friend sent a box with books on grief and grieving. My hands ran over the cover of the words in disbelief that this book was for me. The book was a mirror reflecting the pages of my life I was about to read. This person was obviously familiar with grief and wasted no time in getting tools into my hands to help me heal. Later, I discovered an entire family broke away from their family vacation to be with us the day of his service. It cost them something to tap-in on that day. I reconnected with people I would have least suspected to lean on. Life is funny like that. The people you expect to lean on aren't there, and people you never would have thought would be in your circle become like family.

Everyone wrote heart-touching words, but this note made its way to my wallet the moment I read it. It's been with me ever since. It reads,

Jazz and Matt,

I am without words to fully express what is in my heart. You both and your family will continue to be in my prayers daily. David will forever be in my heart, never forgotten, always remembered. I can picture him running around in my gym class like it was yesterday. There is a part of a song that comes to mind every time I am overwhelmed. "Jesus, Jesus, precious Jesus, Oh for Grace to trust You more. Psalm 16:8- I keep my eyes always on the Lord. With Him at my right hand, I will not be shaken. Love, Karen

Her note reminded me that David wasn't just part of our family but part of the world, part of a community, and part of other people's lives. I know he existed, but some days, my life feels like a dream where it only happened to me, so I treasure it when others remember him with me. She doesn't even know she's part of my tap network.

Then there's Wednesdays. Wednesday became a day of healing and my favorite day of the week. A day where I was seen, felt, and fed, but not just me, my whole family. Laurie, my best friend, has become a sister to me. She understands the code of suffering and taps accordingly. It has been through her consistent love and friendship that I have been restored. She defies my Pentecostal upbringing that says healing only happens at altar calls, with goosebumps and guest speakers. She jumped in the ditch with me and patiently listened, letting me rant, cry, laugh, and eat her food once a week with no expectation of anything in return. Of course, I always try to bring dessert and a side dish, but that's not the point. Being at her house is like the scene from The Shack, where God shows up as a motherly figure. Her gentleness and long, intentional hugs are like heaven, letting me know I'll be okay. Now, let's eat!

Within the first year of our trauma, I could hardly pull myself to do basic tasks. After the meal train and gift cards slowed down, I found myself needing to prepare meals again. What did my family eat?

"Chili? Does your family like chili?" Tammy asks me on the phone, trying to help jog my memory and make a grocery list.

"Yes," I replied robotically.

"What do you put in your chili, hun?" She asks so gently, encouraging me to list the ingredients.

"Um..." I try to recall.

"Do you guys use ground turkey or ground beef?"

"Yes, ground turkey. Thank you." I jot it down. She proceeds to go down the list of ingredients she uses in her chili, making conversation with me as she goes. We finished with the chili ingredients, but she could tell I was still stuck.

"Would you like me to go shopping with you?"

I sigh with relief that I didn't have to do it alone. I could borrow someone else's brain till mine rebooted. "Yes, please, and thank you!" When we hung up, I was supposed to expand my list, but my brain wouldn't budge without an external prompt, so all I had was chili, diapers, and wipes. That's okay;

Tammy came and saved the day. I grab a cart, and Tammy grabs a cart and follows me around the store, asking me what my family needs as we go aisle by aisle, trying to call to mind the way I used to run my house. We talked and joked along the way. I felt like a toddler wanting to just add things to the cart. I wasn't sure if we needed it, but thankfully, Tammy would bring it to my attention. Did I really need green dish soap and blue dish soap? Or advanced whitening toothpaste for dentures? That wasn't really in there, but very easily could have made the cut. My mind was mush. At the end of it all, I had two carts full of food and household items our family needed to start a new life in a different state. It would have been nice to hire a personal chef because my food tasted like grief. It was sad. Very sad. I tried to keep with our Saturday morning traditions of what we call "Big Breakfast." This includes eggs, pancakes/waffles, lots of fruit, juice, and just a big spread of options. Well, one Saturday morning, I'm making a big breakfast. The family sat down to eat, and everything was just awful. The pancakes were either doughy or burnt, the eggs were salty, my home fries were spicy, and I don't even know how because I added no spice that I could recall anyway. The only things that turned out right were the fruit and the Tropicana juice. It took me a few months, but I finally started getting the hang of cooking again. It wasn't perfect, but at least edible.

I began attending a Grief Share group, which I thought was phenomenal. It was a group of kind souls coming together to share our pain but also learn ways to cope. I highly recommend attending a Grief Share. Part of the group's agenda is to go around in a circle, introduce yourself, and talk about your loved one who's passed away. A few seats to my left was a young mother of four who had just lost her husband to COVID-19. Her oldest child was seven, and her youngest was two. My heart broke for this mother who lost her other half and now has to single-handedly raise four children. A few seats down from her was Craig. Craig was in his late 80s and, with a shaky voice, described how his first wife of forty years had died, and now his second wife of four years had recently passed away. He was alone, and his children lived a little distance away. He laughed about how he didn't know what to make himself eat, so he started putting random things together, like ice cream and coffee creamer. Watching this frazzled mom reminded me of myself trying to make the grocery list for chili, and listening to Craig's plight about food gave me an idea. I called my mother-in-law, Wendy, to see if she would join me in making meals for grieving families. We came up with a plan of what type of meals to make based on which ones freeze and thaw well, how many meals would provide a sense of relief without overwhelming us, and finally, the distance we would go to deliver them. Once we got our plan for grieving families together, we decided to make an exception with Craig. Wendy made Craig about a week's worth of meals, all packaged in single-serving microwavable containers for him to enjoy. She couldn't feed him forever, but at least for that week, he remembered what good home cooking tastes like. Wendy and I started a crusade. Our meals included the book "Wholehearted Grief" by Dr. Denise Rollins, journals for kids, 3-5 frozen meals, and 1-2 meal-prep ingredients. At that time, I had enrolled Jacob in a Chik-Fil-A Leadership Academy, and they selected our cause as their community project. They sponsored 40 of these meal packages, which were made by local homeschool students and distributed to grieving families.

Despite having to make our move to PA abruptly, it felt good being around family, and it is a decision I don't regret. Wendy didn't just make and deliver meals with me but attended the kids' graduation ceremonies from Oliva's House, a grief program for teens and children, and attended all of the kids' plays and performances, which helped our kids feel family love and support while they healed. She would send me local events as I learned the area, we would tag-team and minister to grieving mothers, and our weekly drop-ins for coffee and catching up filled my heart, reminding me I have family just around the corner.

Being on the receiving end of love and support has been uncomfortable. My heart is filled with gratitude for every person who prayed, gave, wrote, drove, flew, served, and loved on our family with patience and kindness. We mustn't underestimate the significance of just showing up.

Part of what makes a tap code effective is that each person understands what the other person is going through. New and old friends began to share tragedies that broke my heart for them. They weren't looking for pity, but they communicated: I see, hear, and feel you. I have learned that everyone is dealing with something and needs a tap code.

Professionals

There was a man who prayed and asked God to save his life after his boat became shipwrecked. Soon after the shipwreck, two men in another boat came by and offered the man help.

"No thanks," he said. "I'm waiting for God to save me."

The men on the boat shrugged their shoulders and continued. As the man became more deeply concerned, another boat came by. Again, the people aboard offered this man some help, and again he politely declined. "I'm waiting for God to save me," he said again.

After some time, the man began to lose his faith, and soon after that, he died. Upon reaching Heaven, he had a chance to speak with God briefly.

"Why did you let me die? Why didn't you answer my prayers?"

"Dummy, I sent you two boats!"

I could either ask for help or drown. I reached for every hand I could to stay afloat. I swam to boats and climbed wherever I could. We went to a family counselor, and I had a grief coach, and a counselor who was EMDR certified. I grabbed everything. My religion would have me say, "I don't need anything, but Jesus." However, I call a mechanic if my car breaks down. The church has feared psychology, the study of the mind and behavior, and has encouraged people to steer clear of counseling, therapy, and psychology. Solomon was the psychologist of his day. He studied human behavior and the way people think. He saw "nothing new under the sun" because he noticed the patterns built into nature and humans. Neuroscientists and psychologists have discovered more about the brain and emotions since Solomon's time. Understanding yourself and others doesn't replace God or the work of the Holy Spirit. It enhances the way we engage with others, ourselves, and

God. It can help us become better communicators by giving us perspective and language for our thoughts and feelings. It can challenge us in our blind spots, bringing correction and reconciliation where needed. The right counselor can be a great accompaniment among the multifaceted resources we use to cope with life and live in harmony with ourselves and others. Sorting through your differences in marriage is complicated, and add to that the trauma and loss of a child, and the relationship becomes fragile where the balances can easily tip to either deeper connection and intimacy or isolation and divorce. I had heard about marriages ending after the loss of a child. On the surface, one might think it's because they argue over who is responsible for the child's death, but there are other sources of contention. Grief is a hodge podge of emotions that manifests differently with different people. Men and women grieve differently. In those contrasts, Matt and I had to learn new skills as we navigated visceral feelings we had never encountered. Drawing us closer was the fact that we had the inside scoop on each other's pain, and sometimes, it was that same pain that made us moody and disconnected. Our differing grief responses intensified the next major decision we needed to make. Had it not been for our counselor, I'm not sure we would have compromised in the way we did. We both wanted our family to heal, and we each had ideas on how we felt that should be done. Here's how it all went down.

It was June, a month full of change. It was the month we had boxes all over the house, ready to move when our lease was up in August. We hadn't yet selected a place, so when David passed, we abandoned the house, searched for a new place for a few weeks, and stayed with Matt's parents until we found a place. My husband, his brothers, and our dear friends made several trips to the house, finishing the packing and cleaning. Neither the kids nor I could return back to the house. It was bad enough that the scene replayed in all of our minds every day, but to be there again would be sensory overload. A few weeks might have passed, and my husband wanted move. A subject I wasn't ready for. He wanted to move back to Maryland. I wanted to stay at his parents' house a little longer to gather myself so I could make a more sound decision. I didn't feel like I was in my right mind. He grew frustrated with me, and I grew frustrated with him. Off to the counselor's office, we go. Our counselor helped us find a compromise that acknowledged both of our needs. Left to our own devices, we might have just argued about whether or not to move, but the counselor helped us look beyond the decision to see what the other person is saying they need in order to help them cope. He needed to be moving forward, and I needed to feel safe to heal. We started looking for places in Maryland. We made our first stop at a townhouse. The effects of claustrophobia take hold of my mind, and breathing becomes difficult. I didn't show it on the outside, but I was totally freaking out on the inside. Onward, we go to the next place.

The basement is nice, and the main floor is beautiful, but taking the stairs up to the top level, my stomach grows tight and knotted, and the process starts all over. The kids were silent. I could sense their apprehensions were similar to mine. Their quiet signaled my Spidey-senses. They, too, envisioned the last time we were a family in a townhome together. We get back in the van, shut all the doors, and head back to his parents' house. "What do you guys think?" he asks with some excitement in his tone. Not wanting to shut him down or disappoint him, we all named what we liked about it. "The bedrooms were huge," one of the kids would say. "Yeah, the basement can be a game room." They try to build a vision where we are happy and whole. "I like the kitchen. Those appliances look new." I add.

It wasn't till our next counseling session that I revealed I had panic attacks at each place we visited. The counselor again emphasized both my need to heal and Matt's need to move forward. He challenged us to take the other person's needs seriously and not as an intentional hindrance. Moving to

Maryland was too much for the kids and me because of all the familiarity and triggers we would be inundated with. The compromise was moving to Pennsylvania. If David were here, we'd be in Maryland, but this was the best choice under the influence of grief we could make. I'm thankful for the wisdom and mediation of our counselor, who helped us value one another's needs equally and find a middle ground. Matt drives two hours one way in his commute to work. He makes a huge sacrifice daily that reminds me he cares about my healing. Mourning in marriage is messy and complex, but it is possible to make it through. We were careful not to blame each other, listened to each other speak from the heart, hugged when the other shared tears, and extended grace when we were in moods.

One morning in our new townhouse in Pennsylvania, I woke up feeling completely lost. My brain was empty, and I had no clue what to fill it with. I was supposed to do school with the kids, but I just felt empty. It was like my brain wouldn't cut on. I called Matt to try to put words to this weird headspace. Instead of making me feel inadequate or weak, he said, "Don't do school. Go shopping." I could have hugged him over the phone. It wasn't shopping I was happy about. I'm not much of a shopper, but the fact that he saw my need. I was relieved by his response and felt like I could express myself more intimately with him. He didn't say, "You're the kid's teacher, and if you don't get it together, they're going to fail." He knows his wife. He knows I'm not lazy, and I don't give myself breaks because I take my responsibilities seriously. He understood the difficulty I was having getting back into the swing of things because he, too, was trying to adjust. Seeing each other beyond the to-dos and into who we are and what we're dealing with inwardly brought us closer. Then there were the other moments where we unraveled, hence...the counselors.

Our family counselor helped us pick up the pieces of our faith, marriage, and family. My grief coach, Dr. Rollins, helped me with my trauma, fear of the future, and getting back on the saddle with coaching and, in fact, inspired this book. She truly restored my sense of purpose. After choosing life, she enlivened me again. My EMDR counselor was helpful, but I'm not sure how much. EMDR is an Eye Movement Desensitization and Reprocessing psychotherapy treatment designed to alleviate distress from traumatic memories. My intentions with this therapy weren't only to heal my heart but also my physical brain from the trauma. I had the hopes that I would be restored to my original self. It's hard to tell if it made a difference, but it was worth a try.

Giving Pain a Purpose

America does not have a tradition for mourning like other cultures, making your grief more isolating than it already is. We get a few days of bereavement and back to the grind we must go. Finding comfort, meaning, purpose, and hope can take some time. The process shouldn't be rushed. Jewish traditions give their mourners 5 stages that the community recognizes and honors for the bereaved.

Aninut: Pre-burial

Shiva: 7 Days

Shloshim: 30 Days

The first year

"We must mourn, but we must also set boundaries for our mourning. To not mourn at all, or to plunge into an abyss of grief and remain trapped on its bottom, both of these extremes are detrimental, both to the living and to the souls of the departed."

Americans have no customs to catch us on the other side of our grief. Our jobs and roles await us. We must initiate our own support system and recovery program to heal. As Christians, we bury our loved ones and expect the bereaved to be okay because they are in a better place. I wonder what amount of strength and courage one might possess with the community surrounding them or, at the very least, honoring the deceased and giving place for the survivor's grief for a year. I am not suggesting we need to mimic Jewish culture or that their culture is ideal, but they have something that walks with people during a difficult time in their lives. My friend and mentor lost her husband six months after David passed. She noticed that her large church didn't tend to those suffering from grief. Seeing this need, she felt prompted to start a Grief Share to meet this often-overlooked group of people in her church. Through it, she's been able to fill a gap and touch many lives. People are resilient and have found ways through loss and grief for centuries. Most of those cultures had close-knit communities and traditions where they acknowledged the toll one loss took on the whole group.

I may not be able to change my entire American-Christian culture by starting a new custom, but I have taken the things I've learned about grief and loss to try to help others on their journey. Jessica Dixon, my counselor friend mentioned in Chapter 2, worked with me in launching "A Time to Heal," a free one-day event for mothers grieving the loss of a child, and

"Created to Cope," a four-week group coaching workshop intended to be a pit stop of hope for grieving mothers. Will either of these heal someone entirely? No, but I needed to take the initiative and meet a need. If we each took our pain point and repurposed it, imagine all the people we could uplift along the way. We may not have a built-in way to handle the grief that comes with life or death, but we can certainly encourage one another by tapping in.

Chapter 10

A Life Divided

Death is not the greatest loss in life. The greatest loss is what dies inside us while we live

- Norman Cousins

David is the curtain that divides my life into before and after. I heard people say when they lost their loved one; it was like they lost a part of themselves. It's one thing to hear those words and another thing to live them. Though I am still a mother, I am not David's mother. I lost a role to him specifically. Each child requires an aspect of me different from the others. I was uniquely David's mom. I knew how to save the core of the peppers so he could eat them and their seeds. I knew that spending time with him meant physical activity, and I knew that for him to learn a new concept, he needed a sketch pad to doodle on because it helped him focus better. I knew he always compared himself to his brother and needed extra affirmation that he was doing well. Part of my heart and life was carved out just for David; if I ever wanted to deny him, I couldn't. I bear the marks on my body from carrying him and the lines across my body from delivering him. He is etched into me physically and will always be a part of me, along with his siblings.

The love from a parent for a child is unbelievably strong. It is effortless and unmerited. All the children had to do was exist. I was excited when I saw the plus sign on every pregnancy test, overjoyed with every sonogram, punch, and kick in my ribs. It was love at first sight when the doctors laid my babies on my chest, presenting me with a great gift. These babies, Jacob,

David, Isabell, and JP, are bone of my bone and flesh of my flesh. To earn my affection, all they did was exist. I imagine this must be how God feels towards us.

His love for His creation. His swelling pride for what He's made, hence He calls it "good." I sat one morning on the sofa thinking about my relationship with David in tandem with God's relationship with us. How much He loves us purely because He made us and nothing else, and the heartbreaking devastation He must feel when we do not choose Him in return. Choosing death rather than life. I imagine the way I felt crushed about losing David is the same way God must feel when we are separated from Him. Is this why God grieved in Genesis 6? Does it hurt Him the way it hurts us when our kids turn their backs on us and want to separate forever? When your love is so strong, and then it cuts off without warning, the pain is sharp and sudden. Did God feel this pain when He looked for Adam after he and his wife completed spiritual suicide? They killed themselves, separating not only them but their offspring from being connected to their Creator. It would take centuries to repair the relationship to its original state. Putting myself in God's shoes, I picture His heavy heart prompting Him to be so adamant about our reconciliation back to Himself that He chooses to do something no other false god would have ever done. God's pain turned into purpose when His aching desire to keep us from eternal separation became a grand scheme to get us back. Other gods require worshippers to sacrifice themselves for wealth, gain, and power. However, our Creator came and sacrificed Himself, showing us the way back to Him.

19 "Do not store up for yourselves treasures on earth, where moths and vermin destroy, and where thieves break in and steal. Matthew 6:19 NIV

39 Whoever finds their life will lose it, and whoever loses their life for my sake will find it. Matthew 10:39

Through these verses, we are reminded that He is ultimately our goal and not things. The way back to our Creator isn't to "use" my faith to get all I can on earth and make my life a smooth sail. If that were the goal, that ship would have sailed, leaving me with the reason that my faith in God must be about something more than what I can gain in this life.

If there was something I could have done to save David, even by laying down my own life, I would have done it. And that's the story of God. He's so hurt by the idea of losing us forever that He takes our place so we can live with Him. He doesn't want us permanently apart from Him. Sitting on the couch that day, I felt like I had a taste of God's sentiments and what motivated Him to come to earth. I couldn't fathom taking the pain I felt for David and feeling that same loss for Jacob, Izzy, and JP. To lose all four of my children would crush me. God didn't lose just Adam and Eve. He continues to lose many. If I multiply what I feel by the whole world over centuries, my heart grows heavier, imagining God's immense grief. Grief is that mix of love and anger because there's a fine line between the two. Christ's coming was like God saying, "That's enough! I'm tired of losing my kids. They can't keep dying like this! I have to make a way for them to be back with me. They want to be loved and accepted by the world around them so much that they reject my love for it. I'll go get them myself. I do not crave the things they crave; it will not have the same effect on me. I'll be hated and mocked to show them how to find me. When they believe, they'll do what I do." He comes to earth Himself and restores us to Himself most ingeniously. His plan is multi-layered, using the accuser's own characteristics to boomerang in his plot to save His children. God, put on a human suit and didn't cheat his way out of suffering. Without His sacrifice, I wouldn't be able to see David again, and this would be an eternal tragedy and not just a temporary one. The same way lines across my belly indicate that David was a part of me is the same way the scars on Christ indicate I'm part of Him.

When I am lost, God is not. I lost myself when I lost my son. I lost my passion, drive, and desire for anything this life could offer. Theoretically, I felt like strong faith meant nothing should bother me. If that is the standard for faith, I am very weak and willing to admit my weakness while I pray for strength to carry on. What has changed about me?

Everything. I went from Tigger to Eyore. From life of the party to drawing the blinds. The fun part of me was broken, and my brain was broken.

Befores and Afters

Befores and afters are characteristics you have before and after an event in your life in contrast to one another. It was like I was two different people living two different lives. Jazzmine before and Jazzmine after. The impact of trauma on my brain altered me. It rearranged the chemicals and neural pathways in my brain. From the outside, I'm functional, but on the inside, I'm not me. The executive functioning of my brain had been punched. Planning, organizing, small talk, and even joking became off-color as I felt out of control with my words. I have lacked discipline in areas where I previously held strong principles. Since having my own experience with trauma and all

172

the internal changes, I have wondered how many people don't have a sin issue but a trauma issue. How many people have difficulty getting a grip on the right things, not because they don't want to, but because their spirit has been crushed and their brains have been altered by some event? My trauma was a one-time event. My heart aches for those who experience multiple, repetitive traumas. For me, my brain went on vacation. I wasn't as sharp as I was before. I was more sensitive to pain and simultaneously less patient with people. Every day, I woke up like I was lost, hoping to wake up to a life with David in it. Some nights, I wake up from a dream where my family was whole. I'm not too fond of those dreams. I wake up sobbing in bed, in the shower, or silently on car rides, remembering what it felt like to have four arrows in my quiver.

The aftershock of losing David was discovering I'd never be the same again. "How can you be?" A gentle voice asks me. A friend sitting on the couch across from me hears my eager plea to be who I once was because I don't know this version of myself. "How can you be the same, Jazzmine?" Her question relieves me from striving to go backward and embrace the journey ahead to figure life out now that it's all different. She was right. There's no way I can be the same person. I am different. I'm not better or worse, just different.

"Hello?" Says the person on the other end of the phone call.

My mind now works through the mechanics of a conversation when, before, it was a no-brainer. I had a handle on most American social norms and could employ them without thinking.

"What do I say next? Do they talk, or do I talk? Is this an odd time to cut in? Are they finished speaking?" My mind goes through a dozen questions in the few seconds it takes for someone just to greet me. I've become socially awkward, maybe not to those who don't know me so well, but to those who do. I'm weirder than usual. If they haven't noticed it, I sure do. Losing myself has made me more self-conscious. Sometimes, I want to hide; other times, I want to be seen. I haven't quite figured out the balance or ways to integrate these two parts of myself so I can feel more put together. Still, as time and intention continue, I believe I'll find a space to allow myself to be Tigger when I need to and be Eeyore when sadness overcomes me. There have been times when I've felt like the entire Winnie the Pooh cast. I've been nervous like Piglet, grouchy and worrisome like Rabbit, and wanting to eat sweets all day like Pooh. I had never seen myself swing through such highs and lows till after David.

My issue is wanting only happiness without the other negative stuff; as I mentioned in a previous chapter, pursuing happiness is a snare that will make you even more unhappy because you're not happy. It seems the reality is that we are built to experience both positive and negative emotions simultaneously. The trick is how to lean into both of them in their timing. How can we hold pain in one hand and purpose in the other, suffer but have joy, and feel both grief and gratitude? My misconceptions about Christianity made me feel as though I am only permitted to feel one emotion, and it better be uplifting and victorious. Is it possible to only have joy, love, peace, patience? I'm sure it is in heaven, but I don't think heaven is condemning me for the layered combination of emotions I am experiencing while on Earth.

People tend to avoid people who are heavy and hurting. They aren't sure what conversation to strike. They don't want to ask the obvious questions for fear they may trigger or anger you, so I wanted to be my old self again to relieve people from the duty of trying to figure out how to address my pain. The part of me whose job was to make other people happy. People enjoy your company more when you're happy, so though no one shunned me for my grief, I still felt obligated to crack a joke to keep them around. I wanted Jazzmine back. Her laughter and attention to detail. Sometimes, I want her naive, confident outlook on life. Other times, I was annoyed by her naivety, but I enjoyed her because she was familiar. I want her to bring sunshine and solutions to her friends, not depression and negativity. I have known her all my life, and she's gone. She died when David did.

This brain-altered, weighted-down version is scattered and doesn't always know what to say in social settings; she's stuck sending emails and text messages because words escape her, afraid that her awkwardness will repel people, and she'll be alone. Healing from all of this, for me, meant being who I was before David passed. Being the playful mom, I used to be, the talkative friend, the motivational coach, and the ambitious church patron. Returning to my old self is no longer my goal. I don't want to be talkative, but I want to listen more deeply without trying to find an answer. I don't want to be motivational but find meaning. I don't want to climb church ladders; I want Christ.

"What we do next isn't because David died," my husband says in deep contemplation. "It's because Christ died."

His point is not that we shouldn't grieve our loss, but that we shouldn't get swallowed up by it so that it becomes the center of our lives. It has been a fight to not let grief take the front seat and drive my life.

The grenade that blew up my life didn't take a limb, but it took part of my soul. In the world of grief counseling, they say that the goal isn't to stop grieving but to integrate grief into your life. Grief is not an abstract emotion; we integrate it unexpectedly. It has a deep connection to someone we love. It is the other side of love. David came into this world as part of me because of my never-ending love for him; my love-turned-grief will forever have a space in my life. I am learning that grief is not the whole of who I am. *I am* here learning how to bring all the pieces of me into harmony once again. The only way I can do that is by keeping God at the center.

> *Grief never ends, but it changes.*
> *It's a passage, not a place to stay.*
> *Grief is not a sign of weakness nor a lack of faith.*
> *It is the price of love.*
> *-Unknown*

Chapter 11

Remember

The darker the night, the brighter the stars, the deeper the grief, the closer is God.
-Fyodor Dostostoevsky Crime and Punishment

2021 was the start of a new me. It's far from go-live-your-best-life or you-do-you-boo social media post version. This was far more serious and weightier. I didn't want to return to life as usual or show up inauthentically as if my life hadn't skipped a beat. Life changed drastically. How do we find joy among the multitude of sorrows? How do we stay positive, trudging through all the negatives? I had big questions, most of which would take me my lifetime to conclude, but a new journey has begun.

I sit with a pad and pen in life's classroom, prepared to write my observations and inner thoughts. Writing has brought healing. I'm most honest with myself in my journals. I rewrite the events in detail that took place on that fateful day. I write it as many times as I need to mourn it till finally, I accept it, and its potency diminishes. When you experience something unnatural, it gets seared in your memory. My journal helped me bear the weight of memories so I could sleep at night. I lament each page. You might say it's my own book of lamentations. I lament secondary losses, dreams, hopes, and relationships. I write about new hopes and fresh friendships. I ask, I scribble, I sketch, I create. I separate God from religion and talk to Him straight. I pour my heart out to Him through the ink. I am inspired by King David's diary, noticing he and I share the same sentiments. We both have this mix of thanksgiving and despair. We talk to God, to ourselves, and no one in particular. On the page, we rejoice, trusting God's character, but turn a page, and we feel abandoned and frustrated. King David and I have both contemplated that if we forsake God, where do we go? There's nowhere to turn but back to Him. King David and I are centuries and cultures apart, but the human experience remains the same.

Remember

Asaph, one of David's kinsmen, wrote Psalms 78. It's a long chapter, so you'll have to check it out. He speaks about how God established a testimony in Jacob, but the spirit of the people wasn't faithful to God. They forgot His wonders that He had shown them. The secret to holding onto God in those dry seasons when you're not hearing from Him is to remember. Memory is like a double-edged sword. It's because of this built-in mechanism called memory that I profusely miss my David. I also depend on it to recall the testimony God had established with me before David passed. To keep my spirit faithful to God, I needed to remember. I remember how God kept me from having a serious accident when I was fifteen and driving a friend's car without a permit or license. I recounted the times when we struggled financially, and we would receive bags of clothes or furniture that were given to us right when we needed them. At one point, everything in our house was gifted to us. I can't take David's passing and say God doesn't exist or isn't real because I have a history that proves otherwise. My question, so common to the human race, is, "Why?" Why would God be so faithful to me in all these areas that I would trade to have David back in a heartbeat? Perhaps God knows the heart of man and that even with David, anything I suffer, I would ask God, "Why?" Essentially, I'm asking, Why can't my life be perfect in this dark and imperfect world? To be fair, I look around and see no one has it perfectly, sinner or saint. We can be happy with less or greedy for more. We choose our attitudes and perspectives.

Remembering how God engaged with me despite whether or not I had the right doctrine increased my affection and hope toward Him. I don't know much Aramaic, Hebrew, or Greek to get to the nitty gritty of scriptures. I'm not a historian, so I cannot break down all the Pentateuch symbolism and foreshadowing. I don't know the parallels between the feast days or if we should be celebrating them. I do know that God established himself in my life, reaching me despite all of that.

He Reaches Me

Michael Jackson's thriller terrified me as a child. The music video provoked so much fear in me that I refused to watch zombie movies. The eerie idea of being dead yet alive, because you are mindlessly cannibalizing the living, makes me want to curl up even now. Maintaining a vow to myself never to watch anything zombie-related was disregarded as a street full of zombies appeared in a dream one night. I was chased by one of my worst nightmares. The zombie mob had their dead gaze fixed on me, so I began to run. In a panic, I searched for the nearest building to hide in. I run inside and lock the heavy metal door behind me. I can hear their clamoring thumps against the door, signaling I need to get away fast. Running at full speed down the hallway, I notice the walls all getting smaller till finally, I'm too big, and it turns out to be a dead end. I hear the zombies busting the door in, and claustrophobia sets in. Then, suddenly, out of nowhere, this small space fills with water. I feel my heart racing as I try to think of another way out, but there is no escape. Unable to distinguish between dream and reality, my body responds, and I hold my breath in real life. Just before the zombies break in and the water is right at my nose, the commotion mutes out. A calm voice says, "Jazzmine, you're okay." I wasn't startled or jolted awake. My heart wasn't pounding. It was like those three words had peace in them, and when they weren't spoken to me, they were spoken into me. I noticed the voice didn't use my nickname but my full first name, as if it wanted my full attention. The 'it," I believe, was the Lord. I didn't know it at the time, but traumatic events can cause anxiety, panic attacks, and claustrophobia. That voice. That peaceful voice bypassed my mind and spoke to my spirit. Everything about me calmed. God gave me a lifeline to hold onto whenever I feel anxious. In every elevator, stairwell, or tight space, I pause to replay His voice again, "Jazzmine, you're okay."

God has presented Himself in dreams to me before, but because those were during the time when I was most dedicated, I had attributed God's interactions as warranted. I was fasting, praying, attending church, and volunteering, so in my mind, this was cause and effect. God wasn't talking to me because He loved me but because I worked for it. After spiritually being all over the map, I now know there's not a resume long enough to manipulate God into doing something He doesn't want to do. Knowing that I could be a little off in my doctrine and God still reach me, makes His engagement with me all the more special. He wanted to talk to me despite me not having it all together. He came to visit me, and the only thing I had to offer was a bucket of tears, nightmares, fatigue, and doubt. I was not doing anything special or noteworthy. I didn't ask, beg, or invite Him, yet of His own accord because of His lovingkindness, He brought me peace. Here in this darkness, I've come to know His love for me beyond what I can perform or produce.

He Reached Me Again

One moonlit night a week or two after David passed, I couldn't sleep because the bedroom ceiling made me feel trapped. When trauma and your own mind play tricks on you, your body involuntarily responds. Suddenly, it wasn't just the ceiling that made me feel closed in, but the darkness of the night made me feel like everything was closing in. I stared at the moon, wishing it would turn into the sun. My staring was ineffective and made claustrophobia intensify, feeling the same powerlessness I did when we discovered David. I clicked on the light, afraid to wake my husband or the baby and started writing my anxieties in my journal. To my own soul, I say,

You want the day to come when you want it to come
For the sun to rise because you hate darkness
The impatience you feel waiting for the daybreak reveals your
lack of control over the cosmos.

One must wait with expectancy that the sun will rise again on

its own like clockwork.

I know it's time

It will rise again

And though darkness comes, there's even a light in the darkness

called the moon.

God's provision for us to see in the midnight hour

Though obscure- I still see

Though not as far-I still see

God has made it, so my sight is never completely gone

So, morning or night, still see

Sun or there is still light, and though I wait eagerly for the light

that comes with day, I am never fully without hope. His light is

always with me.

The sun will rise again.

After releasing my panic on paper, I can go back to sleep. The next day, we are on the road to yet another family counseling session. We let music play to entertain us while we are all deep in thought about what today's session will hold for us. I take out my Bible and let the pages fall. They flip and land. I couldn't believe my eyes. It was as if God had responded to my journal entry and my panic attacks the night before. Talking right to me, Isaiah 60:19-20 says,

The sun will no more be your light by day,

nor will the brightness of the moon shine on you,

for the Lord will be your everlasting light,

and your God will be your glory.

Your sun will never set again,

and your moon will wane no more.

The Lord will be your everlasting light,

and your days of sorrow will end. (NIV)

Using the exact same language, God responds that He will be my everlasting light. I won't have to wait for the sun or moon to orbit or the earth to rotate. It was like He said look beyond the lights in the sky. You don't have to wait for daytime to stop panicking; I'll be your everlasting light. What peace this gave me whenever I felt the fear of being physically or emotionally trapped. He gave me a focal point beyond this realm I hope to hold onto and remember in the future.

Jesus in the Ditch with Me

"For we do not have a high priest who is unable to sympathize with our weaknesses, but one who in every respect has been tempted as we are, yet without sin. Hebrews 4:15 (ESV)

Jesus showed his integrity and said He would not ask me to do something He had not done. My savior has experienced what

I've experienced and can comprehend my pain. Jesus' betrayal, public humiliation, and trauma give him credibility to speak about suffering. He's felt it all. He's no stranger to what I'm going through. He, too, has shed tears for the loss of a close friend. (John 11) He, too, wanted a way out of pain and suffering. (Matthew 26:39)

He was an example of how we can endure these things and still make the right choices. He jumped into the ditch of this world with us and got his hands dirty. Jesus didn't control the world around him, though he could have. However, He demonstrated an inner strength that can overcome this world. Overcoming wasn't defined by Him escaping the cross, but that the world didn't subdue Him. The circumstances of this life tempt us to recant our trust in God. Life repeatedly beats us, asking us, "Do you still believe?"

Not being delivered didn't mean God wasn't with me or I did something wrong. Life will not always be fair, but God will always be faithful.

Chapter 12
Redemption

Man can only find meaning for his existence in something outside himself.

-Viktor. Frankl.

In the beginning, in *my* beginning when I was born, there was a void, an empty space where I knew nothing about God. As a toddler, my language began to form, but I still had no concept of God. As a child, I heard songs, fell asleep on pews, and prayed with one eye open. After a dozen coloring pages and lessons, I connected the trees and sky with a Creator called God. As a teen, I learned the rules and parameters of God, the do's and don'ts, particularly the ones about sex, as my hormones rose to test me. I imagined heaven and hell and fought to stay above the flames. I learned that Christ came to show me a better way. He died and rose again, leaving behind the Holy Spirit to guide me into all Truth.

When I became an adult, I collected and absorbed more information to expand my understanding of God. Sometimes, I wished I hadn't been churched because I wasn't just taught a simple message about Christ. Searching for truth isn't easy, but it is simple. I discovered on my spiritual quest that the gospel is for me but not about me. It's like it is, and it isn't at the same time. The paradoxes and pendulum swings are inevitable.

Since David was born, he had been anointed with oil. I prayed over him when he was kicking me from the inside and kissed his face after reading him the stories of King David, Samson, and the miracles of Jesus. I used scriptures to calm his fears and help him navigate through friendships and complicated feelings. We played Bible games to memorize verses like my mother did with me when I was young. Shouldn't this have countered any ideas my son was having about ending his own life? Shouldn't our morning declarations eradicate dark or demonic thoughts? The questions overwhelm and keep me up late at night, shattering the shards of my trust into even smaller pieces.

Ironically enough, the very being that broke my trust is the only one I can trust to heal and restore. I know beyond any doubt that He will help me pull myself together. I know for a fact that he will reach me beyond my error. He knows I've sought after Him but missed Him by miles, yet He sees me for more than my denomination. My cry cuts through to Him even though I'm missing it. Even though I don't know how to worship him perfectly, or going back to chapter six, I can't bring myself to trust the rickety bridge. He still comes to meet me where I am. Here is where I learn about His goodness. I didn't get the miracle, but that alone did not make Him my enemy.

False messiahs and false prophets will appear and perform great signs and wonders to deceive, if possible, even the elect. Matthew 24:24

Many will say to me on that day, 'Lord, did we not prophesy in your name and in your name drive out demons and, in your name, perform many miracles?' Matthew 7:22

Then Jesus began to denounce the towns in which most of his miracles had been performed because they did not repent. Matthew 11:20

According to these verses, should my trust in God hinge on a miracle? If God doesn't, is it all over? Do I stop believing everything I have believed almost my whole life? Is this all a sham if He doesn't? I had been so pumped only to consider one way; that is, the miracle must happen if I am genuinely a Believer. Doctrines then splinter into more messages when it doesn't happen, sending me and so many others on wild goose chases hunting down reasons we didn't get what we asked for. It's like someone got my order wrong at a restaurant, and I want to speak with the manager, or I'm never eating here again, threatening to give them a bad review on Yelp.

What if miracles led people astray instead of closer to God? Is that what the above verses are saying? Could it be that this breaking point has a new perspective within it? Are there gems and rubies waiting to be unearthed in my suffering? Are there nuggets of wisdom in this disappointment? Because God is never absent but ever present, His light is always available to illuminate a way for me to think differently and reframe my sorrows. Could it be that here, in this valley, I meet the lily of the valley? Part of me doesn't want to grow here out of allegiance to my son. To find anything good out of this would feel like a betrayal. But to Solomon, wisdom can be found in the house of mourning.

The heart of the wise is in the house of mourning, but the heart of fools is in the house of mirth. - Solomon Ecclesiastes 7:4

But look at what it cost me. Could Solomon's proverb also mean I mourn because of what it cost me to gain this wisdom?

"I don't know what to believe," I said softly, sitting across from my counselor, who had been helping me hobble along.

"Well, what do you know? Let's start there." He prompts. I take in his question, realizing I don't need to rush. I'm not in trouble for not knowing. Searching my soul for what I honestly believe. This is what I love about going to counseling. I don't have a responsibility to be anyone to him. I'm free to think without trying to uphold a particular image or role. He can see the frustration on my face as I hear copious voices instructing me to follow Christ this way or that way. My counselor doesn't tell me what to believe but gently guides me to rebuild one little piece at a time. His question sent my mind fluttering through all the pendulum swings and gray areas, trying to find balance and truth. I settle into myself and silence all the voices to hear myself think. Here's what I know,

1. God exists and is the Creator.

2. He loves His creation.

3. He's in the ditch with me.

4. I am not alone.

5. I'm open to more.

I treasure the beauty of this simplicity. You exist, you're my Creator, you love me, you are with me, and I want to understand you better.

So, it would seem that my quest has brought me full circle. Or maybe I never left the spot I started in. When I didn't get the miracle I thought something was wrong with me or my faith that God would turn away in my hour of need, but neither He nor I have budged. God is the one I questioned, but He's my only source of comfort. He allowed David to leave this planet after twelve short years but also gave him eternal life. He didn't save me from temporary brokenness yet gave me eternal wholeness.

God didn't give me my son back in the hospital but made a way for us to reunite in heaven.

If I were back at Children's Hospital in that hotel room pacing the floors with JP and Shadrach, Meshach, and Abednego came to my door and asked me, "Jazzmine, you know God is able to save David, but what if God doesn't?" My response to them would be, "He's still God, and there is no other god for me to worship but Him."

Works Cited

Baldwin, James. "The Blind Men and the Elephant."
Americanliterature.com, 2019,
americanliterature.com/author/james-baldwin/short-story/the-
blind-men-and-the-elephant.

Carol Culpepper, Jetta. "Merriam-Webster Online: The
Language Center0011The Staff of Merriam-Webster. Merriam-
Webster Online: The Language Center. 47 Federal Street, PO
Box 281, Springfield, MA 01102; Tel: (413) 734-3134; Fax:
(413) 731-5979; Merriam-Webster, Inc C1999. Free." *Electronic
Resources Review*, vol. 4, no. 1/2, Jan. 2000, pp. 9–11,
https://doi.org/10.1108/err.2000.4.1_2.9.11.

Frankl, Viktor E. *Man's Search for Meaning*. Boston, Beacon
Press, 2006.

God. *ESV: English Standard Version*. Wheaton, Ill., Crossway
Bibles, 2016.

Holy Bible: Good News Translation. New York, American
Bible Society, 2003.

Hone, Lucy. *Resilient Grieving: How to Find Your Way through Devastating Loss: A Practical Guide to Recovery*. Sydney, A & U New Zealand, 2017.

NIV Bible. Grand Rapids, Mi, Zondervan Pub. House, 2011.

"Polymyositis." *www.Mayoclinic.Org*, 10 Aug. 2022, www.mayoclinic.org/diseases-conditions/polymyositis/symptoms-causes/syc-20353208. Accessed 29 Apr. 2024.

"Shock." *The Free Dictionary*, medical-dictionary.thefreedictionary.com/shock.

The Bible: Authorized King James Version. Oxford; New York, Oxford University Press, 2008.

"The Stages of Mourning in Judaism - the Shivah and Other Mourning Observances." *www.chabad.org*, www.chabad.org/library/article_cdo/aid/282506/jewish/The-Stages-of-Mourning-in-Judaism.htm.

About the Author

Since losing David, my husband, Matthew has been willing to do whatever it takes to see his wife and mother of his children back to functioning and thriving. Writing this book as a means of healing was his idea. I'm deeply grateful to Matt for his unwavering devotion to me and our family. Without his self-sacrificing love, I'd be light years behind where I am now. My children, Jacob and Izzy, were stellar kids before we lost David, and even after their trauma, they continue to amaze me with their perseverance and perspectives. I'm so proud of them for holding onto their faith in God. They encourage me in so many ways. JP has kept us all together. His liveliness and meeting new developmental milestones make us laugh and force us to be in the present. We unite when it comes to loving and protecting him. I enjoy spending time with my family and hope to write my next book soon.

www.JazzmineMagloire.com

Made in the USA
Middletown, DE
30 August 2024

59660813R00116